➤ AFTERLIFEFROMABOVE ➤

AFTERLIFEFROMABOVE

Healings of a Paranormal Nature

Anita Billi

For Holly
May you have peace on
your Journey!
Anita Billi

1st Printing, March 2006

ISBN 1-929661-22-3

For additional copies, retail, or wholesale quantities of
this book or other related books, tapes, and CDs, contact the publisher through the worldwide web:

www.TranspersonalPublishing.com

Transpersonal Publishing
A Division of AHU.LLC
PO Box 7220
Kill Devil Hills, NC 27948

Manufactured in the United States of America

1 3 5 7 9 10 8 6 4 2

For John

(1 9 6 2 – 1 9 8 2)

Contents

Author's Note

The experiences recorded in this book represent material I have gathered from an international Internet study on the healing effects of paranormal visitations. Over five thousand stories were submitted to me personally and to the Afterlifefromabove Book Research Group for this book. Out of those stories, I have selected what I thought best exemplified a diversity of common healing spirit visitations.

All stories have been extensively researched and edited for both content and clarity. Last names and the names of children have been omitted to protect the identity of those included in each paranormal account.

Introduction

The Light

"Every man is his own doctor of divinity."
—*Robert Louis Stevenson*

Over twenty years ago at the age of eighteen, I spontaneously received clear insight and an enormous amount of information about the afterlife. I had been resting in the early evening, and began to experience a tingling sensation that started at my feet, and then engulfed my whole body to the point where I was in a state of complete paralysis. Something or someone asked me telepathically for permission for this to continue, and being curious, I agreed. A bright light then entered the base of my feet, surged up through my body, and exploded out of the crown of my head. At that instant, I felt I was a vessel of light that was connected to all in existence. I was shown our connection to one another down to the smallest particles that make up our world. I sensed that the particles were so small that there was seemingly no separation between them. I knew that these particles represented all of us, unified. During this experience, not only did I receive an immeasurable amount of information regarding the afterlife instantaneously, I heard the voice of God. It was at this instant that I understood that the idea that we are entirely separate in any way is an illusion, a falsehood, and that at the core of each of us exists the essence of our common heritage, our creation, from the same cultivated seed of divinity.

This experience of "the light" wakened me to my own soul consciousness—or so I thought—only to find that my consciousness is your consciousness at its ultimate state of expression. I could see that this state of awareness was not physical, and that it expanded beyond measure. This is when I realized that there was no separation between life and death, and that the energy from which we are made has no barrier, or linear time.

Chapter 1

The Definition of Paranormal

"The search for the truth is the noblest occupation
of man; its publication is a duty."
—*Anne Louise Germaine de Staël*

A large percentage of our population today has had an experience that cannot be explained, scientifically or otherwise. These experiences are currently referred to as *paranormal*.

In *The American Heritage Dictionary, Fourth Edition*, the definition of paranormal is simply put. Paranormal events are defined as "events beyond the range of normal experience or scientific explanation."

In my research of paranormal events, I have found that this definition is not precisely true; rather, "events beyond the range of normal experience" *are* experienced every day, by people from all walks of life.

What, then, might be a better way to define paranormal? Perhaps we could say that paranormal experiences are common events, not yet definable by science, and encountered by a large percentage of our population today.

At present, we do not have the scientific means available to prove what lies beyond our five senses, nor are we able to prove paranormal events, such as miraculous healings, often thought to be the work of God. If this is so, and God and the works of God cannot be proven by any scientific means, then I ask, is

God paranormal as well? My answer to this question is *yes*. Under today's current definition, there is no other way to put it.

Human beings like explanations. By living under current standard definitions, we can live a life that assures us some amount of predictability. This is why we have terms and definitions. They help us to define our experiences in life, as well as help to maintain a common order among the populace.

The average intelligence and development of the human race is rapidly changing. Our current technology far surpasses what anyone imagined a hundred, or even twenty, years ago. People nowadays know there is much more to being human than previously thought or imagined. Not only are we growing more intelligent, our senses are heightening. If this heightened state of awareness is now the norm, and experiences that cannot be explained scientifically are happening to much of the population today, then it follows that paranormal events are no longer events outside the range of normal experience.

I invite you to consider that it may no longer be necessary to remain within our current framework of prescribed human behavior, definitions, and thinking. I invite you to allow yourself to consider that paranormal events experienced today are well within the range of normal, and that the current definition of paranormal no longer correctly defines our common, increasingly understood, and accepted experiences.

Chapter 2

Understanding Reincarnation

"I did not begin when I was born, nor when I was
conceived. I have been growing, developing, through
incalculable myriads of millenniums. All my previous
selves have their voices, echoes, promptings in me.
Oh, incalculable times again shall I be born."
—*Jack London*

The concept and definition of *reincarnation*, that of returning to
life repeatedly, is as identifiably unexplainable as the concept
and term "paranormal" itself. The idea of returning to a new
bodily form is currently viewed within the scientific community and general populace as an invalid experience if it cannot
be proven. To believe in anything unseen, the majority of our
population needs tangible, scientific proof.

What is reincarnation, then, if there is no scientific valida-
tion? Reincarnation is being born into a body that you have pre-
chosen before birth. Our pre-chosen circumstances are suited to
match the personal spiritual needs for each of us, as well as to
fulfill spiritual lessons and obligations that we have negotiated
before our birth for each successive incarnation.

If you look to the definition of reincarnation, I believe that
you will agree that reincarnation is a concept that may be better
understood through personal experience and documented case
studies, which repeatedly report the same phenomena occur-
ring throughout the world. This phenomena includes recogniz-

ing others from previous lifetimes who may now be, in this life, a close friend or relative. Also included are remembering past lives, having a vivid recollection of the person you were in another lifetime, as well as familiarity with a place or particular scenes that flash before your memory, and are somehow inexplicably recognizable to you.

Reincarnation offers you the continued opportunity to clear your ethereal spirit of any *karma* you may have accumulated in a past life. Your karma, or the effect of a person's actions in life, can go back lifetimes.

Healing and breaking through the barriers of a karmic debt and clearing your karmic past gives you a new freedom of consciousness that not only affects you but all of humanity. To take it a step further, karma clearing also affects those in the afterlife, because our consciousness is one in the same, and ever connected for eternity.

You always have a choice as to how you wish to work out your karma, that is, anything that needs balancing and restoration in any way. If you have the opportunity, it is wise to clear up any actions now—if you are aware of them, and while in this life and bodily form—that you feel may have had a negative effect upon another, especially if there is something in particular that you are not looking forward to clearing up, or have been putting off for some time now, perhaps even lifetimes. Is there something that causes you mental anguish and deep distress? If so, and if you are looking for a place to begin the process of consciously balancing anything that needs balancing and restoration in any form, then what has just come to your mind may be a good place to begin your karmic work. When you are willing and ready to face all life situations that you have come here to face, every single one, pre-tailored to your own specifications, your karmic opportunities will present themselves to you. You need not do anything. It is perfectly systematic.

When we take personal responsibility for our karmic balance, the whole of humanity is uplifted and feels this change, moving from a state of imbalance to balance. It does not matter if you are experiencing this world, or are between incarnations. All karmic-related actions that uplift in any form and purposely serve to clear undesired past choices are felt at a multitude of levels within our united consciousness.

Many are afraid to cross over into the afterlife, thinking that there may be a significant punishment waiting for them when they arrive. The truth of the matter is, every thought, word, deed, feeling, and intent is seen and felt in the afterlife. When you arrive, you are welcomed with overwhelming love, and there is no judgment, nor is there punishment of any kind. Remember that God—*only loves*, and it is by His examples set by others in human and in heavenly form that we learn this ourselves.

After your death, you are better able to sense your own spiritual essence, your godly essence, and any judgment you continue to hold in any way after death will only be that of your own creation; a creation that you have fashioned to serve your higher karmic purposes.

The main role that karma plays in our lives is to eradicate any separation that we have created within humanity. When your karmic position in life changes and your karmic work at all levels is complete, and all places of past distress are replaced by love, you will have then reached and achieved the metamorphosis from karmic debt to love.

When you have achieved total love in all matters in this life, and all matters within your heart and spirit are understood, and all life conflicts are resolved, you will no longer find yourself returning to a human form. You will graduate from the school of life to another school, one of your choice—a heavenly school for a higher spiritual education.

As many of you may have heard, when we die, we have a life-review. What we have learned in each consecutive lifetime is recorded in the book of life called *The Akashic Hall of Records*. These ethereal records contain every act, feeling, word, thought, and intent that you have ever had during your consecutive lifetimes here on earth, as well as your time in-between incarnations. These records are for review only, and serve the highest spiritual purposes. Many people who carry healing abilities are able to see into this book, and sometimes refer to it without even knowing it. *The Akashic Hall of Records* is our record of evolution. You could say this book is God's personal diary.

In the afterlife, know that names for items need not exist. What is referred to here as "the book" or *The Akashic Hall of Records* is intended to explain something that exists, yet words cannot fully describe, nor can the human brain completely comprehend, the depth and importance of the information held within these timeless recordings.

We can be confident in knowing that throughout our many consecutive incarnations, our karma, our lives, and lives after this life, are well planned to the very last detail. After death, we again experience the opportunity to review how well we contributed to eliminating any separation we may have experienced with others in life. This is the intimate and ultimate goal and role of reincarnation.

Chapter 3

⟶ *Spirit Communication* ⟵

"The lights of stars that were extinguished ages
ago still reaches us. So it is with great men who
died centuries ago, but still reach us with the
radiations of their personalities."
—*Kahlil Gibran*

If we want to learn about spirit communication, we must first understand the principal mechanisms used by those in spirit who can, by adapting and changing their rate of vibration, communicate with us in almost any way imaginable. If we can understand what spirits are made of, we can better visualize the ways in which they use energy in order to appear.

Spirits are composed of molecular energy and are able to communicate by increasing or decreasing their molecular structure and rate of vibration to match ours. It is as simple as tuning a radio to find a clear station. Once a common energy frequency is matched, spirit communication is clear and easy.

When we call upon those in spirit, for them it is as if we are speaking through the amplification of a microphone. When our call is heard, a spirit travels faster than the speed of light, and appears in an instant. This accomplishment is met with great ease for those who are no longer confined to a physical bodily form.

Visitations come in many forms. Often, they come in the form of the familiar scent of a loved one, even though they are deceased. Why does this happen? This happens because traces of the molecular energy pattern of a person, their personality and soul essence, remain after a visitation. This is most commonly felt as a "presence" in the room with you, combined with an aroma that permeates the air. Included are scents of specific perfumes, cigars, and particular cooking aromas, even though no one may be cooking. I call these traces of molecular energy patterns *imprints*.

Imprints are derived from the energy of who we were in past lifetimes. To each current lifetime, we bring our imprints from past lifetimes. These imprints are useful in helping us remember others whom we have met along our many incarnations. When you meet someone, and you feel you instantly know them in some way, what you are really doing is recognizing their collective imprinting, or traces of a past-life experience that you have shared with another. In many cases, these feelings arise when people have spent several past incarnations together. This is the memory and consciousness of *collective imprinting*.

Collective imprinting is like a memory bank that continually contributes to your spirit identification and lifetime history account. All consecutive lifetime experiences are deposited automatically and there are no withdrawals. Remember, your history account, or *Akashic Records* account, is an open-book account, always available for review by others both here and in the afterlife.

The ultimate purpose of collective imprinting is not only to recognize those whom we have known from another lifetime, but also to be able to identify our very *first* imprint, the God-seed within each of us, carefully cultivated by the hands of our Creator. For this, we must first see the God self in our own selves. This happens naturally, when we are ready, and we know when it is happening when we are seeking information that will lead us into a deeper insight as to who we are, and the importance of our lives. If we seek the true nature and the wisdom available to all of us, we will come to realize that life is not always seen from the perspective of the human eye. Life is something that can also be felt deep within, something continual, something divine that can never be extinguished, our spiritual motivation toward the truth in all matters and our spiritual light.

Spirit entities are able to appear in many different forms. Often they appear as shadows, which disappear when looked at directly. These shadow type of spirit appearances are best seen by using your peripheral vision. This type of spirit contact often includes telepathic thought transference whereby information appears in your mind from sources outside yourself. This experience is known as *telepathic communication,* whereby one entity communicates to the other, without using words. What is used are sounds vibrating at different rates, pulses, and pitches that speak in tones that assimilate into the human brain as pictures in the mind. Most of the time, these sounds are inaudible to the human ear.

Other common spirit appearances come in the form of a bluish-white light that can emanate in any shape. This light is like no other and actually allows you to see spirit energy moving before you. This type of spirit visitation is one of the few types of spirit appearances that you can look at directly as well as walk though.

When walking through a spirit entity, you can expect a tingling sensation accompanied by the feeling of a merging. At this point, you do not feel completely yourself, but rather, feel merged, one soul with another soul, as your molecular energy combines and vibrates at the exact same rate. In order for this to happen, a spirit will slow their molecular rate of energy frequency, matching their frequency to yours.

In order to make appearances, spirits can easily utilize light and electricity. I have found this most common among spirits who have newly departed. Upon visitation, a spirit's light body emanates a flickering light very similar to that of miniature

Christmas lights, and is usually accompanied by an expanded feeling of love that fills the immediate vicinity. This is what I personally experienced when my grandfather passed away.

My grandfather passed away in 2001 at the age of ninety-five. At the time of his death, I was sitting at the computer desk in my home, writing the beginning of this book. On my right appeared lights that I could see out of the corner of my eye, at about the height of a tall man. When I looked directly at these lights, they disappeared. When I would look back to the computer screen, they reappeared, and it was as if brilliant Christmas tree lights were gleaming on and off, and on again. This continued for about forty-five seconds, with my looking at the lights out of the corner of my eye, and then . . . my grandfather was gone. The feeling was unmistakably him, and I immediately called the hospital where he was, with a nine-hour time difference (at 2:30 a.m. his time), and the nurse who answered the phone told me that my grandfather had just passed away. I then called to notify my family that he was gone. I will never forget the remarkable visitation, the lights and abounding love that surrounded me and assured me that life, without doubt, continues.

Other remarkable spirit appearances are the appearance of orbs. These spirit appearances take the shape of a sphere, and often seem as if they are spinning. These spinning orbs are able to dart around a room faster than the eye can follow, and are commonly silver in color, but can also appear clear, or any color the spirit, appearing in the form of an orb, desires.

Orb visitations, like light visitations, are also accompanied by an expanded feeling of love, and often, a picture-impression of who it is that is visiting.

Orbs are becoming more widely accepted by the scientific community because orbs can be photographed, and often have been in the past—though sometimes not on purpose, and often without the knowledge of the photographer.

There is much debate as to the validity of a photograph containing orbs. Some say the orbs may be dust; others, water spots or chemical blotches; but then, there are some photos that you can look at, and it is undeniable. You know, see, and feel that yes, you are looking at a photograph of an actual orb, a spirit, captured within a compacted ball of spinning, floating energy.

I have had the experience of seeing an orb and was amazed at its velocity and maneuverability. This silver orb, luminescent in color, was spinning in such a way that it left trails of what appeared to be silver fog or smoke, very similar to the look of dry ice. It hovered in front of me for about thirty seconds, and I would say it was the size of a baseball. Then the orb seemed to communicate with me telepathically, and I was told to get a pencil and paper and begin writing. A second later, the orb was gone. Thus began my introduction to automatic writing, where I uncovered several past lifetimes, and opened communication with those in the afterlife in a way that I had never done before. It was as if I had somehow plugged into a main source, a freeway of knowing.

Automatic writing is a fascinating way of communicating with spirits because it allows you to be a passageway for incoming information, in the form of energy, coming from another place other than the mind of the person who is doing the automatic writing.

Automatic writing is allowing yourself to sit quietly and write the first thing that comes to your mind. It does not matter what you write and it is best not to think about anything, if possible. Automatic writing allows spirits to communicate messages to you, and not only do spirits communicate, but also your personal spiritual guides. It is important to remember when you are utilizing the technique of automatic writing that you need to continually protect yourself from information that comes to you that may not be for your higher good. It is also vital to learn to discern between spirits that are of a good nature or of God, and those who have joined in, networking against the will of God. This is where you need discernment to distinguish between what is correct and what is incorrect in all actions and situations presented in life.

Other spirit visitations include a spirit who chooses not appear at all. Though you may feel their presence, their choice may be to communicate through telepathic means. You will have an interruption of thought, and flashes of a different train of thought will enter your mind for no apparent reason. You may wonder why you are suddenly thinking about something different, and most often, you will immediately be able to relate what you are thinking with a person who now resides in the afterlife.

What happens when unwanted spirits, spirits unknown to us, visit? If you find that you are having a consistent spirit visitation, consider for a moment the possibilities as to why that particular spirit is visiting. The mere fact that a spirit is coming to you indicates a close connection to that entity. An entity may be part of your spirit family, or a deceased family member who is asking for your help. What can you do? Helping to heal a spirit, if you are able, is essentially what is happening when you choose to help an entity. Not only are you helping a spirit in need, but also you are helping them to move closer to total unification by helping another spirit become liberated from anything that binds them. This binding of the spirit not only occurs in life, it can also occur in the afterlife.

Imagine if you will that you are in fact connected to everything in existence, and that every act, thought, and word affects the whole of all that exists. With this in mind, if you so choose, you can help a spirit entity simply by asking what it is that they would like you to do, just as if you were asking a friend. You can do this in your mind, or out loud. Your answer will come immediately, and you will then know what it is you are to do. Always listen to your first answer. This answer is from the part of you that is directly connected to the wisdom of the universe.

Not all people can communicate with spirits. It is for no other reason other than that they may not be ready for such an experience, or, somewhere within their personal spiritual beliefs, they do not yet recognize that we do continue to live after we die and continue to communicate in immeasurable ways.

Chapter 4
❧ *Visitations* ❧

"The best and most beautiful things in the world
cannot be seen or even touched.
They must be felt with the heart."
—*Helen Keller*

Spirit visitations are very common occurrences that can happen at any time to anyone. How do you know when you have had a spirit visitation? It is something you feel with your innermost being. Even though your conceptual mind may have a difficult time adjusting to the presence of a spirit entity, your ethereal being knows the messages of the unseen and their validity.

The most pronounced spirit visitations come in the form of dreams, thoughts, shadows, orbs, lights, ectoplasm, touch, smells, sudden room temperature changes, visual appearance of spirit beings, and electrical appliance disruptions.

Electrical appliance disruption requires a special talent and is caused by a spirit entity who utilizes and manipulates the variables of available atmospheric electrical currents at the molecular level. A sudden halt in molecular atmospheric movement can cause a sudden drop in room temperature as well as flush electrical circuits with erratic energy patterns. This causes irregularities with anything electrical, namely, telephones, lights, and entertainment appliances. In addition, there is the natural planetary energy (the magnetic energy of the planet) in conjunction with atmospheric energy (energy from the atmosphere) that spirits utilize in order to harness energy. This energy becomes a vehicle for spirit visitations.

Ectoplasm is another common spirit appearance whereby spirit entities, by collecting molecules from the natural electromagnetic energy of the earth's atmosphere, make appearances by utilizing this energy to create shapes. Ectoplasm can appear as a fog, a mist, or similar to smoke. In photographs, it appears the same, and often includes added streaks of movement and light, sometimes including color.

Common among pronounced visitations are visitations in dreams. The dreamer may not be certain, in a waking state, that they have had an actual spirit visitation. Often, the experience is thought of as "just a dream," or is entirely forgotten and is never discussed with anyone.

Sensing another in your presence, or feeling the touch of another, even though you are certain you are alone, is not frightening by any means, and simulates a soft breeze. You will feel a warm presence (even if you are outside and it is cold) and perhaps a touch upon your physical body. When you turn to see who it is, you will find that no one is near you. This is what happens when a visiting spirit touches us, yet does not appear within our visual field of perception. Nevertheless, spirit appearances, no matter how they appear, can hold the same amount of intensity and ability to heal as any other type of visitation.

It is not unusual, during a spirit visitation, to receive a vivid representation of a spirit visitor's age, and know what they look like down to the smallest of details. This is easily achieved by not looking directly at the spirit entity, but rather by looking at them out of the corner of your eye. Most often, this is where spirits appear, to the left or right of you. If you try to get a better look at an entity by looking directly at them, they often disappear. The reason an entity may disappear is that when we try to focus on a spirit entity optically, we break the connection of communication that has nothing to do with physical form, and all to do with seeing at a molecular level. What does something look like at a molecular level? When you see dust in the sunlight, that is what seeing at a molecular level looks like. What you are seeing when you see a spirit at the molecular level is actual energy, slowed in its molecular makeup, to the point where it becomes visible to you.

The easiest visitation for a newly departed spirit to make is a visitation directly after death. This is because the earthly essence of a human being has not yet gone through complete transition and ascension, from a bodily form to an ethereal being. Frequently, a person who has recently died comes in spirit form to say good-bye in any way they are able, especially if their death was unexpected. If this is the case, it is not unusual that a newly departed spirit stays within earthly boundaries until they are completely aware and comfortable with their recent transition. This also allows them time to adjust to their new ethereal or heavenly light body.

In cases of a violent or accidental death, it often takes some time, from our perspective, for the total and complete ascension of the deceased. Know that in these cases, those who are not fully aware they have crossed over are under the loving care of guides while in this transitional phase, from life to the afterlife, and are taken care of completely, as if they were a newborn.

When a person dies, they may be in disbelief and/or in denial due to the nature of their death, and may not be in complete understanding that they have died. When a physical departure is abrupt, a person's spirit can become jolted from their body excessively fast, and they may be unaware that they have crossed over to a new dimension. In such cases, a presiding spirit guide or angel, depending on the circumstances, comes to the rescue and aid of any person who is in distress. This is what many now term a *spirit*, or *soul rescue*.

Both angels and spirit guides perform soul rescues. The difference between the two is that guides have chosen to assist you throughout consecutive lifetimes, and angels arrive moments before impending death to assist you during your death, especially if it is unexpected. Angels can also prevent occurrences, such as premature death, by appearing to you and offering you a glimpse of a future event that you may wish to avoid. These events tend to include experiences beyond the normal experience of a natural death, including suicide, or death by the hands of another.

Afterlife rescues do not happen at the onset of the after death state. Rather, a person is encouraged to find his or her own way. When this becomes detrimental to the spirit in any way, a rescue then occurs.

You may not necessarily feel the presence of an angel, or spirit guide, but may feel that something is different. You may feel a comforting, equivalent to arms surrounding you in warmth and light, in your moments of deep grieving or distress.

Spirit guides and soul rescuers provide and ensure an environment for those who have crossed over and find themselves in distress. This environment is very similar, if not exact, to the same surroundings a person experienced in life. The soul rescuer, who will stay with the disincarnate entity until they realize that they are in another dimension, and out of bodily form, re-creates a temporary setting of the person's previous life environment. It is then, and not before, that they will be ready to move forward from the state of unknown death to the known and once again remembered state of the afterlife.

Often, a person who has just crossed over makes simultaneous visitations immediately after their crossing. This is whereby the deceased spirit is able to visit their circle of family members and friends at the same exact time. This accomplishment is easy once a person is released from the confinement of their physical body.

In our human state of awareness, time appears essential to us. For most, it is almost impossible to conceive that time does not exist in the afterlife. This fact, whether we can conceive of it or not, makes it possible for spirit, without limitation, to be in many places at the same time, because our human spirit experiences our world from the perspective of one, all-inclusive, and without limitation, or time. Think of time as transforming to energy, vibrating faster than the speed of light. This is what happens to us when we die. We transform to pure energy and can immediately utilize this energy for the purpose of visitations. In addition, we see that measurement, of any kind, is non-existent, and that we are indeed infinite in all ways.

There is a point that a person reaches in their spiritual evolution where they can experience everything, including the past, present, and future, simultaneously and at multiple levels of consciousness. This is the natural state of the afterlife and is one of many stages of enlightenment.

Many think about dying from the vantage point that life and the afterlife are separate worlds, when in fact, life and all it consists of are simply a part of the continuing evolution of our own spiritual growth.

When our spirit enters the afterlife, we find that the pleasure of being able to convey love to another, even through unconventional means, such as spirit visitations, is one of the gained abilities for those who have recently entered back to the spirit world. This is especially wonderful and surprising for those who were incapable of showing love in their last human incarnation.

When we arrive in the spirit world, nothing is secret. In the afterlife we find that all that we ever said, our actions, and anything we have ever thought of, is immediately known and seen with clarity. Not only is this clarity seen through your own consciousness, it is seen throughout the consciousness of all, like an open book. Any wrongs that occurred in life become clear the moment a person exits their body and enters into the spirit world.

Upon arrival into the afterlife, spiritual advisors assist you, preparing you for future incarnations. Spiritual advisors help to ensure that all wrongs experienced from past incarnations are opportunities for corrections in future lifetimes to come. This opportunity, our karmic planning and repayment opportunity, is by choice. When you elect to choose your future life programs, it is with the help of several spiritual advisors who urge you, in all ways, to grow and evolve to your highest capacity.

There is no need ever to wonder what your highest capacity is, as it is ever changing, and one day, you will have fulfilled all evolutional goals in life. You no longer will have to work at attaining your highest possibilities by right action, correct thinking, and clearing up your karmic debts. You will have already accomplished this.

Remember, there are no mistakes in life, only opportunities to learn and make corrections. If all actions were already in total alignment with our creator, you no longer would have a need for subsequent incarnations.

One of the most important healing aspects of our own death is that we once again have the opportunity and ability to view our lives, and all that occurred in them, from a vantage point of our capacity to love completely. Our growing awareness of the availability of pure love provides the desire within to set up future human conditions and experiences designed to balance and correct any action, or actions in life, that were anything less than love. As we move closer to this pure form of love, both in life and in the afterlife, we bridge all gaps of separation.

When we face our own deaths, or the death of someone we know, our personal consciousness expands to another level of heightened sensitivity, and our perceptions of death may alter. We may become more open to unconventional methods of thought where life after life is concerned, and may unexpectedly wonder, even surprising ourselves, if we do in fact continue living in some form after our death. We may also question if those who have died before us are still among us.

After-death visitations are immensely healing. Though we may still carry a great deal of pain and grief associated with death, it becomes easier to release our grief once we know and can see for ourselves, sometimes for the very first time, that those who have died are still able to communicate with us.

Many people have the experience of knowing when someone is about to die, or has just died. In many cases, they receive a sign and know instinctively that someone they know is about to cross over, or has already.

Directly after the moment of death, even though thousands of miles may separate you from a person, it is possible to feel an expansive amount of energy and a presence that goes far beyond what we thought we could see, know, or ever imagine. This energy and presence can sometimes cause phenomena such as normal household items moving on their own, falling, or breaking, as well as telephones ringing, but no one is there. Also included are alarm clocks (without batteries) going off and clocks stopping at a particular hour. These experiences, however unusual, are in some way comforting because somewhere inside, you can feel the presence of a spirit visitor, perhaps someone you know well, and the reason for their visitation.

When we experience after-death visitations, we find that there is a great assurance within the visitation itself. This allows us the freedom to move from extraordinary pain and grief to understanding. This assurance and understanding can bring a significant and immediate insight into death that not only soothes the pain we associate with grief, but also allows us to embrace a new way of looking at death.

In the following story, Therese shares with us her experience of a spirit visitation from her best friend Lanette, who came to say good-bye shortly after death. What we learn when we read this story is that Therese recognized the moment of her friend's passing, even though they were separated by a great distance.

The Last Visit
by Therese

When I was growing up, I met a girl named Lanette. We became the very best of friends. She would tell me her secrets, and I would tell her mine.

As I grew older, I fell in love with a wonderful man and eventually married him. He lived in the country quite a long way from my hometown, so I had to move and leave my best friend Lanette behind. We always kept in contact with each other either by phone, or letters, and once in a while, a visit.

One day I got a letter from Lanette, and it was very bad news. She told me that she had not been feeling well for quite some time, so she went to see her doctor. Her doctor took all kinds of tests and found out she was a very sick woman. He told her he could not do anything for her and that she had approximately one year left to live. I cried my heart out when I read this letter.

Not many months after, while I was cleaning house, I heard all my jars, which I kept in the cupboard for my preserves, break. It sounded as though they all fell over and broke into pieces. I didn't know what was happening and thought maybe my cat had gotten in there and knocked them over, but no, my cat was sleeping on my bed. I went over to the cupboard and opened the door. To my surprise, the jars were all still standing and not one was broken. Just then, I thought of my friend Lanette and could feel her presence.

I hurried to the phone and called Lanette's place. When I asked how she was, they told me that she had just died a little while ago. That is when I realized that the sound of my jars breaking was to get my attention, and that Lanette had come to say good-bye. I will miss her and know that when my time comes, she will be there waiting for me.

Author

Visitations directly after death not only bring immense healing to our grief and loss in a deep and personal way, they allow us to consider the possibility that life does continue in spirit. Direct after-death spirit visitations teach us that we are more than just a body, and that death is merely releasing what we no longer need, a physical vehicle, for the purpose of continued growth and personal spiritual evolution.

How does an after-death visitation feel? An after-death spirit visitation often feels very pure in a way that is not easy to describe if you have not experienced it. The best way to describe the purity you feel is that it is like the sudden capacity to feel pure light energy and abounding love in a way that changes you forever. After a spirit visitation, you cannot help but remember the moment of pure love that you experienced with such strength and will that you literally feel healed just from the spiritual nature of the visitation and presence of spirit energy itself. It is as if those who are visiting us directly after death are bathing in light and holding the hand of God.

In the following occurrence, Pat shares her description of what it is like to have a visitation in the form of lights that resemble miniature Christmas tree lights. While driving her grandmother's car home from the hospital, Pat was visited by a luminescent, out-of-body passenger.

The Drive Home
by Pat

My grandmother was very dear to me and I always let her know it. When she finally died, she was ninety-nine-and-a-half years old and had baked cookies the day before she had a major stroke. The whole family was devastated. Yes, we all knew the math, but it still did not stop the pain.

When I left the hospital, I got into the car she gave me, which she had driven for years. On the drive home, she appeared to me right there in the car, as miniature sparkling lights, which filled me with love and an awesome feeling of peace. All she actually said was, "It is all right, Pat." I never shed a tear after that, because I knew she was right.

Author

When we experience a spirit visitation, especially directly after the death of someone we know and love, we also experience a type of communication that on one level may be new to us, yet on another is somehow familiar. This communication, one of the many levels of communication available to us both in life as well as in the afterlife, is *telepathic communication*; a level of communication that is utilized by those in spirit who form their energy into words and picture impressions for you to receive in your mind, just as if someone was talking to you. These picture impressions can be especially insightful when death comes unexpectedly, as was the case with Michael and his son, Billy, who communicated with his father directly after his death, and continues to visit him today.

My Billy Boy
by Michael

My son Billy came from California to visit me in Colorado after four years of our not seeing each other. His eyes were bright and clear on this visit, sparkling.

During this last visit, Billy and I talked, as fathers and sons do, and hiked all around the new home I had made in the Rocky Mountain front-range. He loved the home in which I lived, a multi-remodeled quaint little 1910 house set deep in a canyon.

The house was in a very small, 1890s town at the foot of Pikes Peak. Out of my back door, a trail led to another trail that brought you directly to the top of the famous mountain. There was verdant foliage, evergreens, wildflowers, vast mountain views, and wildlife galore.

Billy had grown up in the Los Angeles suburbs. Now we were enjoying the wild flavor of the Rocky Mountains together. It was a wonderful experience. We walked and rode our bikes on the many trails every day of what would be his last visit.

The loss of my son was difficult, grievous, and at the same time enlightening. Billy was a powerful person. It wasn't until after his death that I realized just how powerful he was. He came to me so strongly that it increased my awareness of the after-death state. I became more secure in this knowledge because of his visits. Spirits in this time of transition can exert some definite force at the earth level in a very strong, personal sense.

Billy drowned in a motel swimming pool on his way back home to California. Presumably, he had a seizure while swimming early in the morning. Two young men were talking at the other end of the pool, and noticed him dive in. They continued talking, and by the time they got up and looked at the bottom of the pool, it was too late. Neither dove in to help. One went to call 911 and a passer-by on the second floor of the motel ran down and dove in to attempt a rescue.

I drove to the funeral home in New Mexico where Billy's body was. I had called ahead from my home to have his body cremated, and they said it would be done upon my arrival.

When I arrived, the proprietor was very apologetic. There had been a helicopter crash and he had nine bodies brought in during the night and couldn't get around to my son's body. "Please forgive me," he said. "We'll have it done in forty-five minutes; the body is going into the oven right now." I walked outside, astonished, speechless, and in shock. This was all too much. As I walked out, I saw the beautiful blue sky, a few white clouds with silver linings, and I heard the oven ignite and roar into flames. I went and sat in my car and listened to the roar. Billy sat next to me. I had chills . . . and I laughed. We laughed together! He was there, in feeling and spirit.

In forty-five minutes, the funeral director walked out with the plastic box that contained what used to be my son Billy. He apologized again. Billy and I left.

I was sure the police report would be ready by now so I drove to the station and the desk sergeant gave me the report. I also asked him for a copy of the coroner's report, and a death certificate had to be ordered.

While reading the report, I found, or rather I should say that Billy "showed" me, an error. The officer on duty suspected drug involvement in Billy's death, and again another rush of chills came over me. These chills seemed to be Billy saying, "No, not true." Later this was to be confirmed by the autopsy. I felt as if Billy were talking directly to me.

Upon my return to Los Angeles with the ashes in a plastic box, Billy's mother and I arranged for a memorial service on the beach. We contacted as many of his friends as we could and had them meet us at the beach along with all of our family.

I placed the ashes in the center of the circle of friends. We all held hands around. I explained that we would each have a turn around the circle to say a few words about what Billy meant to each of us. I was surprised by what they said. These contemporaries of his loved him. He had become their baseline, their wisdom, and their teen-guru.

Billy was twenty-eight when he died. His knowledge of his own spirit had given him wisdom beyond his years. Apparently, enough wisdom that he knew that he would live beyond the death of his body. When we all had our say around the circle, I took the ashes to the tip of a rock outcropping and poured them into the swirling wash of the waves. This is of course illegal in the state of California. We don't want all those ashes washing around with the oil and sewage in the water— ha! It seemed fitting that the actual end of his physical existence should challenge the existence of silly laws.

Billy was such a Don Quixote for causes and outdated laws. In seconds, his ashes became part of the great ocean of the earth. I cried.

Years later, I saw the movie *Good Will Hunting*. Quite unexpectedly, I cried for an hour. My son was so much like the main character, he even looked like him. He had passed seven years before I saw this movie, quite coincidentally on exactly the same day and date. I did not realize this until the next day.

Billy was the son from my first marriage. My first wife and I are on very good terms. I still love her, and she still loves me. We were just confused kids when we divorced. We were struck very hard by his death, of course, but both of us somehow had a feeling that he would die young.

It is only occasionally that Billy comes to see me now. At first, after his death, I felt his presence many times. Looking back, I feel that he was there whenever I needed him and that his spirit would come when I called, so to speak.

Shortly after Billy's death, my meditations were full of his life, and my days were full of memories of our times together. I believe he came to me each time I thought of him. The tingles still come, as I believe he does. It is as if I am his view of this world. He comes because he likes to visit me, and to see my sights, and to live my life along with me. These are all just feelings I can't explain very well. My intuition, my tingles, and my insides tell me when Billy is with me.

About five years ago, I went to a "Psychic Fair" in my hometown where there was an aura camera. I meditated and thought of Billy before I had my picture taken. There he was, right over my left shoulder, a ball of blue-green light. I have seen these balls of light during and after meditations on several occasions and thought of him immediately. When I see these balls of light, I feel like it is Billy's spirit visiting.

Author

Losing a child at any stage of a child's existence is not only unforgettable, but it touches you in a way that makes you especially aware of the importance of life, and the time we spend with our children, even if it is only for a very short period.

If you have lost a child and can still feel their presence, know that you are not making it up. Although great pain continues with the repeated thought of the loss of your child, and you feel certain that you will never get over it, perhaps looking at death in another light may be helpful. See that any amount of time spent with your child, and then the coming of their passing, as an opportunity to move into a new energy available to you both, an expanded energy that has only changed into another form. I can best describe and compare this energy in the afterlife to the Theory of Relativity by Albert Einstein, where $E=mc^2$. That is, E (energy) $=m$ (mass) times c (the square of the speed of light). I interpret and apply this theory to the afterlife, in that when a person crosses over, their *mass* (now changed) is able to go faster than the speed of light in the form of energy. You could say it backwards and say that c^2, the speed of light squared, when applied to m (mass; our physical bodies), converts into E, equaling energy. In other words, when a person dies, their physical mass converts into an energy that is beyond measurement.

Some of us do not experience spirit visitations, and we may wonder why others, and not us? The reason for this is that perhaps you are looking for a sign so diligently that you are unable to feel the subtleties of a visitation. This does not mean, however, that you will never be able to have the experience of a spirit visitation. It only means that at this time, you may not be ready to recognize the subtle energy changes that occur when a spirit visitation is within your immediate presence. Often, it takes a profound visitation for a person to recognize and adjust to the finite energies used for the appearance of a spirit visitation.

For those of you who have had the experience of a spirit visitation, you now know what the presence of a spirit feels like. Those who have not yet had an encounter with a spirit, or perhaps have not recognized that you have, know that it is possible for you to do so. You have only to be open to receive like a radio receiver. When the dial of the radio is turned, you can easily tune into any station or *frequency* you desire. When we allow ourselves to be receivers of our desires, our life changes, and we begin to see that our yearning to connect with those in the afterlife is fruitless, as we are already connected, and have been for eternity.

Chapter 5
Crossing Over

"Everything science has taught me strengthens my
belief in the continuity of our spiritual existence after
death. I believe in an immortal soul. Science has
proved that nothing disintegrates into nothingness.
Life and soul, therefore, cannot disintegrate into
nothingness, and so are immortal."
—*Wernher von Braun*

The timing of our death is already determined before we ever
enter into physical incarnation. The one who makes this deter-
mination is you, in conjunction with higher beings, assistants
purposefully sent by God, who are deliberate in showing you
the choices and lessons available to you for future incarnations.

When our time comes to cross over, the crossing will go as we
have planned previously to this incarnation. For many, the difficult part of facing death is not knowing if what we believed
during this life was true and correct. Perhaps we may never
have practiced a faith at all, and maybe we never even believed
in God. So what is it like to cross over when we have such an
array of beliefs and disbeliefs? It is different for everyone and is
according to what a person believed while living. If we can remember that we are superb creators, we can see that worrying

about what is to come—which, again, is already planned out to perfection—is not necessary.

One must try to remember that death is an illusion, a perception, and what appears to be "death" is actually the birth and transformation of the human spirit back into the afterlife. For most people, it is an accepted fact that our physical bodies die. The part of dying that is difficult for many to accept is the false impression that we cease to exist after we die. We may dare to ask, "Where does our soul go after our death?" The essence of the person's spirit, the soul that temporarily resides in a physical body, transforms and is everywhere at once. The person after death is actually more alive when this change takes place than they ever were in life. If death is looked upon this way, as a transformation, then we can be assured that each physical incarnation is one of the many stepping-stones on our journey to discovering the expansion we experience the moment we venture from our physical bodies.

In this current time, many are born with an innate feeling, a pulling, to go home. Often, for some, this feeling is persistent and continues to become stronger. People go through the motions of life, but frequently are never satisfied by the containment they feel, the sense of being encapsulated in a human body. For those who recognize this feeling—and you know who you are—perhaps you are here to help guide others back to the place from which they came, a place of light, creation, and love. It is also a sign for you that your time of incarnating to earth is near completion.

When you are facing your own death, know that just before death occurs, there is a lifting of the spirit, so to speak, and you become lighthearted and accept death with an ease that you never thought possible. Often this happens with the help of guides and departed family members, who come to assist you in any earthly matter still important to you.

For those who may be facing a painful death, know that close to the moment of crossing, the essence of who you are, your spirit, is lifted from your body, and you will experience no pain when you are dying.

Where physical trauma is experienced, and the pain seems greater than ever thought imaginable, know that a natural morphine is released into the body, and no pain is felt. This happens in the cases of those who survive a great trauma of any kind, or serious physical injury. Those who do not survive escape any pain associated with death by leaving their physical body before death is pronounced.

When crossing over to the afterlife, you will immediately regain a lightness of spirit. So much so that right before your death, you may encompass new ideas that might possibly go against your previous religious beliefs.

In life, you may have observed a particular religious faith that did not deal with the afterlife, thus not preparing you for your own death much less the death of another, which is often more difficult to face than your own.

What happens when we die? Shortly before death, a person becomes fully alert. He or she may open their eyes, sit up, and begin to speak, or look as if they see something that is not visible to others. Those who are very weak, and even those who have been unconscious, will also have a renewed life force, become alert, and even speak. These are, in part, preparations for leaving the human body.

What happens to us when we leave our human body? The energy molecules of the spirit begin to speed up in preparation for transition and exit. Just before crossing over, it is very common for a person to mention that others are there in the room with them. When these ethereal visitors arrive, shortly before death, they are seen in accordance with the spiritual beliefs held by the person who is dying in order to be of the greatest assistance during the crossing and transition process of death.

At the time just before physical death, we are assured by our spiritual assistants that life does continue in spirit. If necessary, we are offered glimpses of the afterlife, a gentle reminder of our residence while out of body. These glimpses are of a welcoming nature, and assist us in preparation for the understanding of all matters concerning the nearing death of our physical body.

Sometimes we may forget that the religious circumstances we may be born into can greatly influence our beliefs where the afterlife is concerned. This is why gentle reminders are necessary. They help us to remember that ultimately, we ourselves approve of every birth, as well as every death, while in our ethereal residence and afterlife state of consciousness. This renders not only the gift of learning and experiencing our evolutional progression, but also serves as a constant reminder to us that we always have freedom of choice.

The following story is about a woman, Brinda, who was with her mother at the time of her mother's death. We will see from Brinda's description of her mother's last moments that we indeed are not alone when we die. In addition, we will see that there are those who do assist us in all matters concerning our lives, and our approaching deaths . . . our guides and escorts home.

My Mother's Deathbed Vision
by Brinda

My mother had been in and out of hospitals over the last year, near death at each admission. She was coherent and not delusional. She had congestive heart failure, and lung and kidney cancer spread throughout her body.

One morning in the hospital room, about 2 a.m. when all was quiet, my mother stared out the door of her room and into the hall that led to the nurse's station and the other patients' rooms. I said, "Momma, what do you see?" And she said, "Don't you see them? They walk the hall day and night. They are dead." She said this with quiet calmness. The revelation of this statement might send fear into some, but my mother and I had seen spiritual visions many years prior, so this phenomenon was not a shock for me to hear about, nor for her to see. I, however, did not see them myself this time. This short conversation was not mentioned again.

My mother's surgeon said there was no point in treatment as the cancer had spread throughout her body. He said she might have six months to live, at the most, maybe three. So I brought her home to die.

My mother passed unexpectedly four weeks later. The night of her passing, she was restless and anxious. Although my mother was a spiritual person, she had been in denial throughout her illness and declining health. She did not want to die, therefore, she would not acknowledge the prognosis or her condition. She always talked as if she were going to get well, making plans for things to do in the coming spring.

At about 7:30 p.m., she asked to be carried out to the enclosed front porch. It was winter, and cold. But she insisted, and by this time, I would not deny my mother any request. I wrapped her in blankets and made her as comfortable as possible. My mother was an invalid and could not support herself in any way without help. A few minutes before 8 p.m., she said, "I have to go. They're here. They're waiting for me." Her skin glowed, and the color returned to her pale face as she attempted to raise herself and stand up. Her last words were, "I have to go. It is beautiful!" And she then passed at 8 p.m.

Several months later, the alarm on my clock went off at 8 p.m. sharp—on a clock that was broken and had no batteries in it, which had been set for 6 a.m. previously. I could feel the presence of my mother and her amusement at achieving such a task and bringing it to my attention. A year and two months to the day of my mother's transformation, she appeared standing in my kitchen as whole, healthy, and young. I was surprised, knowing she was dead, but so happy to see her. We embraced in a hug, and I said, "I love you." And then she was gone. She had come back to say a final good-bye and let me know that she was happy and okay. I know my mother is finally home and at peace.

Author

Just before Brinda's mother died, the energy molecules of her spirit began to speed up in preparation for transition and exit from this world. This is why those who are very ill and very close to the moment of death will become bright and have color return to their face. Not only did Brinda's mother regain a healthy physical appearance, she had a renewed energy within her that made her want to stand up for her departure when she could not even walk, and go with those who had come to assist her in her crossing, to a place where she was both ready and eager to go to.

If we listen carefully to the inner voice we all have, we do get glimpses of our own deaths as well as that of another's death to come. Usually, if it is someone close to you, it is that person who thinks of his or her death first, and then this thought is transferred to others through a unified innate telepathy. To put it another way, all thoughts, when thought of, are transferred to the one, or global, mind. When death comes seemingly unexpected, all events leading up to a person's death can and do appear as a type of synchronicity. Know all along that these events are indeed preplanned, before this incarnation by each individual. Recognizing that someone is about to cross over, or knowing that someone has just crossed over, is natural, and is a part of ourselves we may want to pay attention to more often. Our innate wisdom not only aids us in situations where death is concerned, but also helps us to understand unforeseen events and the synchronicity in which these events take place.

In life, we often see a chain of events as synchronicity. When we become aware of this feeling associated with specific happenings, we know we are in tune with higher energies. Within the experience of higher energies comes a knowing, a communication, and a remembrance of what is already deliberately planned.

On many levels, as we shall see in the following account, Liz was aware of the events that were unfolding before her eyes. Not only was she aware of the seemingly odd events transpiring, she participated, at first unknowingly, in the preparations for the departure of her father, whom she saw disappear behind a veil to the other side during an eerie thunderstorm.

Loss and Synchronicity
by Liz

The one most significant factor that stands out regarding my dad's death in 1998 is the certain way it was played against a backdrop of synchronicity. There was a strong sense that the whole sequence of events, however distressing at the time, were preplanned, and that love can indeed reach across mysterious divide between life and death.

When I last spoke to my dad from Heathrow Airport, where I was preparing to board my flight, there was a heartfelt farewell tone to his voice, as if he were subconsciously tying up his good-byes to his family. I remembered thinking at the time that this was unusual behavior for Dad, who generally didn't like communicating by phone and would avoid answering it whenever he could. I must add that my dad always suspected his passing would be very sudden, in the tradition of both his father and grandfather.

My dad died of a heart attack while I was on holiday with my sister on the island of Cyprus, so the news hit us like a bolt from the blue. The night before, my sister and I, sharing an apartment in Paphos, had been intermittently kept awake by an eerie thunderstorm, not something I had ever experienced there on all my previous visits. We both felt extremely uneasy, though we could not put our finger on why. For one brief moment I could have sworn I spotted gossamer strands of light hovering briefly by the ceiling, but I dismissed this as a trick of light. I now believe this was the veil slowly lifting between this world and the next for my dad, and that I momentarily witnessed this unfolding. The moment we discovered that he had passed away, as the shock was filtering in, I distinctly recall feeling the physical sensation of someone hugging me, and I instantly registered, "It's Dad."

On this trip to Cyprus, I had decided, with Dad's permission, that I would arrange for a new wedding ring to be made up for my mum, since she had lost hers some years earlier. Oddly enough, it was during the time between placing the order for the ring and collecting it from the jeweler's that my dad passed away. So when I returned home and gave the ring to my mum with my dad's name, Ralph, and the date of their marriage endearingly engraved on the inside, this gesture took on a particularly poignant meaning. And yet at the same time it seemed so very significant, like a consoling sign from beyond the grave from my dad to Mum, a sign somehow set in motion before he died.

It is the sum total of these events—the "links in the chain," as my dad used to say fondly about synchronicity—the healing and *knowing* element shown to me during that period that most definitely bolstered my belief in an afterlife, extracting a glimmer of a predestined sense of our departed loved ones being but a whisper away.

Author

In life, we often see a chain of events as synchronicity. When we become aware of this feeling associated with specific happenings, we know we are tuned into the higher energies always available to us. Within the experience of higher energies, there comes a knowing, a communication, a remembrance of what is already deliberately planned.

We may ask ourselves at some point in life, "What happens during the transition when our physical bodies die?" This question can be answered by many who have had divine experiences, or by those who are at a stage in their spiritual evolution where they simply *remember*. Here is what I remember, and my explanation.

When we die, we go back to the place in which we existed at the beginning of our creation. During meditation, I saw the beginning of creation. I saw a man in deep meditation. The quiet was profound, and the state of awareness and energy I observed encompassed all of creation. It was the calm before creation, just moments before we existed.

It is my belief that this is why so many people meditate in one form or another. They are trying to reach that part of themselves felt at the time I have spoken of, the beginning, when God created our life form.

When we cross over, we are offered a new perspective of our life and are able to evaluate it, without judgment, and decide where any further corrections are necessary within our perspective of who we are. This profound and newly remembered awareness that comes just after death invites us to reevaluate our evolutional progression. Once we arrive at the point of evolution where this new awareness becomes known to us in life, and no longer needs to be seen from an afterlife perspective, further incarnations become unnecessary. We then graduate, so to speak, to a higher education where we utilize our advanced awareness and, in many instances, become guides ourselves. This progression evolves in countless stages until we one day ascend, in totality, to the place from which we came. It is at this time that we will return to pure love in both expression and being. We will completely remember from whence we came.

Chapter 6

⇒ *Difficulties Crossing Over* ⇐

"We can easily forgive a child who is afraid of the dark;
the real tragedy is when men are afraid of the light."
—*Plato*

There are many reasons why a person may have a difficult time crossing over. Some reasons include experiencing a sudden and unexpected death, the inability to accept death, the love of material wealth, unfinished earthly commitments, lack of faith, fear of the unknown, and love for those we are leaving behind.

Death is a great shock to the spirit awareness when it comes unexpectedly. Car accidents, falls, and the like remove the soul from the physical body in one swift instant. Often, the person who has crossed over is blinded to their guides and tries desperately to regain life and to reenter their physical body. They become fixated on this one task and lose sight of the reality of their death. They stay alive the best they know how, and that is by visiting or hanging around those whom they knew and loved in life.

The love of material wealth is high up on the list of reasons a spirit does not go to its rightful place after death. In this case the person who has crossed over will continue to re-create the same surroundings as they experienced on earth. They have a wonderful time doing this because every creation in the afterlife is easily accomplished with a single thought.

When the acceptance of death is difficult, those who are un-aware they have died will be aided by spiritual assistances who help them to rebuild their previous comfort zone or home sur-roundings, wherever they felt most nurtured, and continue like this until they are able to understand that they no longer have a physical body. Should the afterlife state carry on too long, and it is determined that spiritual advancement is not taking place, help arrives in the form of angels and spirit guides.

Unfinished earthly commitments weigh heavily on the spirit of those who have crossed over and are in the final stages of their departure. This is common for those who have had an abrupt and tragic death. Often these people never had the op-portunity to reconcile upsetting or emotional events that oc-curred in their life. This not only causes spiritual disturbances, it also has a great impact on spiritual growth and well-being if it is not understood that anything seemingly unfinished in life can always be worked on from an out-of-body state.

Lack of faith and the fear of the unknown also slow the pro-gression and ascension of one's spirit being. Though it is natu-ral to have fear of the unknown, if we think of the unknown in another way, that we have created our future just as we would like it, then we can be certain that what we think is the un-known is actually something of our own creation.

Crossing over is a great relief once you leave your physical body. You are weightless and can travel faster than the speed of light. You are able to see, with a vast perspective, all the things that you did not understand while in your latest physical form.

Immediately after death, any lessons that were not learned in life will be in clear view for your review. If you so choose, you then have the opportunity to make any corrections you believe are necessary. In most cases, making these corrections will re-quire additional physical incarnations.

The reason that it takes more than one incarnation to learn a lesson already known and seen in the afterlife is that we are made to forget what it was we were to learn once incarnated. If we remembered, there would be no need for additional incarnations.

Unless all earthly attachments, as experienced in human form, are released at the moment of death, a person who has just crossed over will remain in a place of lingering. Often, this is the case for those who take their own life, or die a sudden and unforeseen death. If this happens, those who have died are offered an environment that reflects that of their previous comforts, similar to or exactly as they had experienced on earth. This period does not last long, and for some is a necessary part of the transition phase from life to the afterlife state of consciousness.

Addressing any part of our life or death experiences that does not allow us to live fully, both in life and in the afterlife, becomes necessary for spiritual advancement.

In some cases of accidental death or suicide, a person's soul becomes jolted out of their physical body and remains in a place described by those who have been there as "the blue." After much research into this common experience, I have come to find that "the blue" represents an atmospheric condition of the spiritual body at a molecular level. After the body dies, the energy of a person begins to transform, but then the transformation stops and remains incomplete. This is because the transformation of the ethereal body was premature, and the person who died did not live the life that was to prepare them for ascension after death. In other words, their transformation had no destination. In these cases, a person can remain in "the blue," a place just above the earth's atmosphere, until a spirit rescue occurs.

If you are somebody who has experienced a visitation where you receive, in some fashion, information concerning someone who has died and is in "the blue," then you are probably the best person to help them as they have already made a connection with you from the spirit world.

The spiritual consciousness of a person during death is often in a state of shock until it is released. Spirit-release often happens on its own, though sometimes it requires the help of a spiritual medium who can easily see the condition of a disincarnate being as well as help to liberate them from their unforeseen circumstances.

Hypnotherapy, whereby a person is induced to a sleeplike state and experiences forgotten experiences, can also assist a person by addressing any issue that may be buried at the subconscious level. These issues include uncovering previous lifetime memories that may be causing distress in this current lifetime, as well as helping to identify just what is preventing a person from living fully.

When we think upon death from a spiritual perspective, I think the most distressing part for most people is the thought that you might end as you now know yourself. On a physical level, the thought of not breathing is difficult for some, and for others, it is the moment when you actually will exit your physical body. On the soul level, we know instinctively that death is actually a birthing into our continued existence.

Through our many earthly incarnations, showing love to our fullest capacity is not always an easy task. When recognizing this in life, it is always wise to remember that you have created *all* situations in your surrounding life that offer you the opportunity to love to your fullest possible capacity. When you cross over, you will immediately see how well you transcended all opportunities presented to you in order to move closer to love.

What is important to remember during your life? One of the most important questions you will be faced with is "How did you make others feel?" It is not the personal gestures toward others in life that matters in the afterlife, though they are valuable lessons in giving. What matters is how others receive your gifts. In other words, are you giving for reasons that are focused on you, or are you giving for reasons that truly focus on giving to another?

When you give of yourself, make certain that you are giving for the benefit of someone else and not yourself. Otherwise, giving then becomes an act for one's self rather than an act of truly selfless giving. This is because the act of truly giving comes from the deepest act of love. When you truly give, in love, you are closing the gap of separation. By giving and loving another selflessly, you are actually loving and giving to yourself when you see that this idea comes from the perspective that we are all one.

Most difficulties in crossing over originate from the inability to forgive yourself for what you will immediately see when you cross over. With this in mind, it is wise to begin practicing forgiveness so that you may swiftly learn to forgive yourself in any situation or circumstance that may arise and prevent you from a complete transition into the afterlife.

Chapter 7
The Other Side

"For nothing is hid, that shall not be made manifest;
nor anything secret, that shall not be known
and come to light."
—Luke 8:17, *Holy Bible*

I believe that there is not a person alive who has not wondered, at least once in their lifetime, what it will be like for them after death. Questions may arise such as, "Do we continue to live in some form after our life?" and "What happens to our soul and spirit when we die? Where do they go?" If we want to answer these questions, we first must answer what our soul and spirit is.

Our soul is the immaterial entity that survives death. This means that the soul has no body or form. Our spirit is the animating force and the drive within our living beings. Our soul and spirit are inseparable, for you cannot have a soul without having the animating force, the spirit that motivates you at the deepest level of your continuing existence. With this in mind, we see that there is no separation between our soul and our spirit, and that our soul and spirit are the sum of who we are.

The soul and spirit may appear as if they are separate when you are alive, and this is, in part, the motivation for progressive incarnations. When we can see and learn that the spirit and soul are not separate, and that the idea of life, and all experiences had in life, are created to assist us back to a point where separation of any kind is nonexistent, we can better understand the essence of our being.

Just before we die, we become aware that we are not alone and we feel the inviting presence of our spiritual guides who assist us, if necessary, during our journey from life to the afterlife. When the moment of death arrives, we can expect to feel a great freedom, a release, and a lightness of being that may be very much unexpected. Moments before your crossing, all pain is released from the physical body as well as our ethereal being (soul, spirit, and entity of who you are combined), and you then are able to take the position of watching your own death. At this time, you will not be alone, and will have those who have gone before you with you, assisting you in letting go of your earthly, bodily presence. Sometimes this is not as easy as one imagines when you still have one foot in life, and one in the afterlife, and are at two places at a single moment where you can still feel the emotions of those in life who are in attendance at your deathbed.

We are often drawn to wanting to stay in life simply for the sake of others, but we know instinctively that this is not correct. It is then that we allow for a complete release of our human body as we take our last breath. Once we are out of physical form, our method of movement changes immediately, and we are able to travel faster than the speed of light. At this time, we often take the opportunity to visit those we love and let them know we have successfully arrived into the spirit realm.

You may wonder, "What do you do in the afterlife and how long do you have to stay there before you can be reincarnated again?" Many attend something very similar to what we call a school. There are schools in the afterlife and lessons to be learned just as we have here on earth. School is not a punishment by any means; it is looked upon favorably, and is a way to accelerate your spiritual growth, if you so choose. What can you learn? The answer to this is what haven't you learned? These will be your major subjects to consider. The choice is always yours, and if need be, your personal assistants—spiritual guides and teachers—will help you to decipher your highest and wisest option for your afterlife studies. These studies often include reflections of past lives as well as projections of future lifetime choices that will serve to maintain the highest discernment possible, maximizing your conscious growth by way of energy flow and light.

Some of the most difficult lessons are those experienced here during our earthly incarnations. It takes constant attention and care, attending to and being responsible for your physical body. In the afterlife, you have no physical body; therefore, your attention becomes focused upon your ethereal body, which strives to maintain constant balance, and continuously gravitates toward a pure state of complete consciousness.

Another choice in the afterlife is to simply rest. Why rest? The purpose of resting is for assimilation and absorption of previous lifetime experiences. These resting periods greatly depend on the degree of difficulty experienced in one lifetime, or many lifetime lessons combined.

It is much easier in the afterlife to reflect upon life's lessons with clarity, as our awareness is naturally at a heightened state after death. At this time, many may realize they have completed their personal work on earth. If this is the case for you, you may be offered a position aiding those who are in need of your assistance, both here on earth and in the afterlife, if this is not already the work you are doing currently. This work can take on many forms. We can choose to become out-of-body guides, assisting others who are in bodily form as well as those in the afterlife, or we can choose to become lifetime guides who serve a single person throughout many successive incarnations, and are present at each death. We can be keepers of children and play with them until they realize they have crossed over. We can be anything we wish in the afterlife. Our work, both here and in the afterlife, will always match our ability and wisdom, so we never have to worry about choice. When choices are presented to us, we always know instinctively which choice is for the best.

We now have among us obvious spiritual masters in every corner of the world who have incarnated here to assist in the spiritual evolution of man. These people have agreed to incarnate at different locations throughout the world in order to be of direct service to mankind. If you take a moment, you will realize that there are many spiritual leaders near and available to you. They are of all religions in order to capture the widest audience, as it does not matter which road you take toward enlightenment. What matters is that you arrive.

There are no secrets held in the afterlife. Those of you who thought you had kept anything in life well hidden may be especially surprised to find that everything you ever thought of, said, or kept secret is an open book for all to see. The reason it is so easy to see another's spirit in the afterlife, and in life as well, is because we have developed the ability to do so. Helping us is the understanding that we are of one entity. We are of one consciousness, and in this conscious state, we are able to connect with the infinite knowledge and wisdom available to guide us always.

If you are unsure that there is an afterlife and feel concern for yourself, or perhaps a loved one who has passed before you, you are in for a most splendid surprise. When you cross over, your loved ones appear immediately.

In the heavenly plane of existence, our loved ones know everything that is happening during our lives here on earth. Often, they will appear to you before your death to let you know they are there to assist you with your crossing when your time comes. Those who have never seen a spirit entity before may see them just before death when the molecular activity within the physical body accelerates. It is at this time that we are able to feel and see the presence of our friends and relatives in spirit, as well as our spiritual guides. We will also feel a heightened energy, at the molecular level, which enables us to connect with those in spirit whose energy is vibrating at the same rate and energy frequency as ours, in order to communicate with us.

When we die, it is a homecoming, just as a birth is here on earth, but with more splendor. There is whatever one's heart desires, no limit, and no end to beauty and creation. Best of all, you remember once again that you really do have free will in all that you create, and the results are immediate.

When we are born, we go through a much greater shock than death itself when we find that we have reincarnated back to into this world, especially if we reincarnate back to earth soon after death. The reason it is such a shock is that we often temporarily forget our afterlife capabilities while in bodily form, such as the ability to speak without words, travel faster than the speed of light, and create anything we desire by simply applying our thoughts to our proposed creations. The surprise of it all is that we do not remember what it is that we are forgetting. This is why people are increasingly unsatisfied with life and continually strive. It is in our nature to strive because we are trying to reach and remember that place that we know exists, where our capabilities are limitless, just as we are limitless.

Why do we forget how to use heightened abilities when we reincarnate? We lose these heightened abilities because our human brain is not capable of processing and integrating information as we do in the afterlife. Ultimately, we are not meant to remember our past lives and time in the afterlife, because what we are here to learn is to stay present in every moment, focusing our energy on our soul evolution rather than regression. There are cases, however, that do require regression into past lives in order to let go, or to heal a part of ourselves that is not in the present moment.

I have always seen the afterlife as our true home. In life, just as it is hard to say good-bye to friends and relatives when you have visited and are going back home, so it is the same when you cross over. It is bittersweet and you may feel sad to go, but at the same time, there is another feeling, a welcoming accompanied by a *knowing* that there is so much waiting for you when you reach the other side.

Chapter 8

About Apparitions

"It is the secret of the world that all things subsist
and do not die, but only retire a little from
sight and afterwards return again."
—*Ralph Waldo Emerson*

Spirit entities are able to produce shapes and forms by using the
amount of energy available to them at any given moment, and
for any given reason. Spirits consciously are able to slow their
energy, the molecular movement within their energy field, so
that they can become dense and visible to the human eye. This
density creates a spirit form also known as an *apparition*.

Apparitions, or spirit energy, can make appearances by utilizing the materials available in the immediate vicinity. The
range by which a spirit can make appearances is great and without limitation.

Apparitions appear for a number of reasons and often carry
special messages to those who can see them. They leave you not
only deeply touched by your experience, but often you are
filled with an abundance of love accompanying the visitation.

It is not uncommon for people who have recently died to re-
produce themselves as they appeared while living. When this
happens, those newly in spirit form will show themselves as
they appeared at the peak of their health in life. They do this in
an attempt to assure you that they are fine and have indeed
completed their crossing.

The first appearance of an apparition can often be frightening for those who are witnessing it. It is important to know that spirit energy cannot harm you. It can, however, be shocking, because we have not been taught about spirit appearances as general knowledge. Now that the general population is moving closer to understanding the presence of spirits, we can better accept the possibility that each of us is rapidly gaining an understanding of the finite energies utilized by a spirit for communication, a communication that extends beyond this life.

In the following story, Gary appears to his sister Jill, who was at his bedside when he died. After seeing her brother rather comically appear to her behind a Spanish lace shawl, Jill could take comfort in knowing that all was well, and that her brother Gary was undeniably in peace. Her grief was lifted.

My Brother Gary
by Jill

Shortly after the death of my brother Gary, I was sitting on my bed reading and felt something in my room. I looked to the left and saw Gary's profile through a purple Spanish-lace shawl that hung from a nearby window. This happened less than two weeks after his death. Gary died in August 2002 from a brain-degenerating disorder called Creutzfeldt-Jacob disease, a variant of mad-cow disease.

When Gary appeared, he let me know he was okay in a way I could easily accept. I was appreciative of his appearance because for me, the way in which he had died was unsettling. I was afraid that he was not at peace and not able to complete his life due to the swift destructive nature of his disease.

I was there for Gary's last few breaths, with him looking into my eyes. Now I know that Gary is okay and at peace, and I see him more now than when he was alive! He continues to fulfill his promise to me that he would visit me after his death.

Author

When death is sudden, or a fast-working degenerative disease takes a life, we sometimes find ourselves in the position of never being able to say good-bye. This is why an apparition visitation can be so healing, not only for our mind, but also for our grief at the deepest level of our being.

Most often apparitions appear in order to deliver a message. Even if you do not recognize who it is who is visiting, or anything about the apparition itself, more often than not, you will receive a message that enters into your mind at the instant of the visitation.

In the next story, we learn that apparition visitations can be suggestive of a future to come. Tina experienced the sudden appearance of a woman who, in spirit form, offered a glimpse of a future event concerning a neighbor who was dying at the time.

An Apparition
by Tina

Late one evening, I was looking into the neighbor's yard at their driveway and saw a small puff of grayish smoke. It started off as a ball and lengthened from top to bottom. I saw a woman with a cloak over her head, like the ones they wore back when there were horses and buggies. She took it off, looked at me, and shrunk back down into a ball—and poof, she was gone. It was only for a matter of seconds that this all happened. I was sure that it was a message. My neighbor was dying, and I figured that the cloaked woman was letting me know that death was coming. He died a few months later.

Author

Tina's experience of an apparition visitation is a wonderful example of how spirits utilize energy to make appearances. In this instance, what Tina saw was a spirit, who gathered the available energy within the immediate vicinity, and slowed the energy to the point where it became visible to the human eye. After an appearance, it is easy for an apparition to disappear because spirits travel within an energy field that moves so fast, it is almost indescribable, in both human distance and speed.

Once a spirit entity is ready to disappear, it will release the slow-moving molecules that it took to make them visible. In an instant, it will be gone, and you may wonder if you ever saw anything at all! This is a common feeling after an apparition visitation, and many find themselves searching for an answer to exactly what it is they saw.

It is common for a person who has had a visitation to talk about it extensively. This often happens because visitations open you to a new energy that is both fascinating and exhilarating. However, when you discuss your experiences, you find that others might not understand exactly what you are talking about, and may even think you a bit unusual. When this happens, we often retreat into our safe thinking and old beliefs, casting any paranormal experiences we have had to the wayside.

When we hear children tell of the appearance of apparitions, we often react as if they are making a story up, hoping to disperse any fear we feel our children may have experienced. This approach, though we may think it beneficial, often discourages a child from discussing future spirit encounters. Nevertheless, if a visitation has made a deep impression, it will never be forgotten.

In the following story, Therese recalls a memory she had as a child while sitting with her brother watching a fire on the land behind their house. After the roof caved in, an apparition of another roof appeared, and later turned into a little girl and a dog. Both the girl and the dog stayed long enough to be seen by both Therese and her brother, and then they disappeared.

A Strange Cloud
by Therese

My brother and I saw the weirdest thing when we were about seven and eight years old. Around 8 p.m., we were in bed for the night when we heard a fire engine stop near our house and saw flashing red lights on the walls. My brother came running into my room to tell me that the small apartment house on the land just behind us was on fire. There was no one living in the apartments at the time because the inside was not yet finished being built.

Being kids, we got very excited. Our mother came up and told us we could look at it if we stayed quiet, then she went back downstairs to go outside with my father to watch.

As we watched the firefighters running around trying to put out the fire, the roof of the building caved in. About five minutes later, a big white cloud came out of nowhere, made itself flat, and settled on the building as if it was putting a new roof on. Then about fifteen minutes later, this cloud-roof rose up and there was a perfect shape of a girl sitting on it with her legs crossed in front of her with her hands on her lap. Kneeling right behind her was a boy with his hands on her shoulders, and a big dog lying beside them. Then this cloud slowly flew off in the opposite direction from the smoke.

We told our mother what we had seen and she said that she hadn't seen anything. Maybe we had a better viewpoint from the second floor, or my brother and I had a very good imagination.

Author
Children are able to decipher spirit visitations much more easily than adults due to their open-mindedness. As Therese's story shows, she has remembered this experience since she was a child, and is very certain of the events that happened on the evening of the fire. It is only later in life that she questioned her

experience, which is very common when we remember our experiences from an adult perspective.

Often stories that include spirit visitations and seem out of context, such as spirits who appear in a new or unfinished dwelling, may be indicative of a prior residence located at the same site where new construction is taking place.

Sometimes, spirit visitations do not bring an immediate message, but rather are visitations in preparation for future events whereby the person or persons who experience the visitation gain added ability and knowledge to be used later in life to communicate with those in the afterlife.

Apparitions are sometimes known to cause uneasy feelings, not only because something appears to be there when there is in fact no one around but messages may come with a warning type of feeling that is accompanied with discomfort. This is often true while in the proximity of the living quarters of a spirit that prefers you not to be there. Often, these spirits are in great need of healing and release. Anger can accompany their spirit energy, making those who enter the dwelling feel as if they are not welcome, especially those sensitive to spirit entities.

Dolly shares with us her experience of entering a home where she immediately felt uneasy. So uneasy, she never went back again. This story presents a perfect example of spirits who have not yet ascended to their rightful place. Not only do they refuse to believe that they have died, but also they may be confused and refuse to leave their created comfort zone. This comfort zone can be the place where the person once lived, or near people whom they loved, or both.

In Dolly's story, she tells us of a house she visited that had two disincarnate beings who hung around the dwelling causing discomfort for the people who lived there and their friends.

As you will see, a man and a woman, both spirit apparitions, often appeared from the waist up to the residents of the house Dolly was visiting. It is important to note that though some may view appearances such as this as a ghostly prank, in most cases, it is not. It takes an enormous amount of energy for spirits to appear, and this is why they may appear as an incomplete bodily form. When we understand this, our fear of apparitions diminishes.

Ghosts in the House
by Dolly

I used to use the CB radio a lot and had many friends on it. One of these friends invited me to visit them at a house in our town. They spoke of having ghosts in the house. It interested me and so I went to visit them and stayed for about an hour. It was a quaint little two-story house, probably about 150 years old. They walked me around showing me the place.

We went to the kitchen and sat at a table. We were talking when I started to get a real queer cold feeling in the pit of my stomach. I actually started to shiver and asked if anyone else was cold. No one else was cold but me. I asked them about the ghosts, and they told me about them. They said they had two ghosts, a man and woman, who loved to play pranks. They would walk up and down the stairs, but you could only see the legs or the upper half of them.

The night I was there, I did not hear anything but kept getting colder and weaker. I was to the point of outright freezing when I finally told them I needed to leave.

I later called a friend who knew a spiritualist minister, and she came to visit me. I told her of my experience, and she told me that I was a natural medium and all the ghosts wanted to do was to make contact through me. She told me not to be afraid, but that was easy for her to say and hard for me to do. I never did go back to that house.

Author
When you come across any situation where you feel uncomfortable with the presence of spirits and you want to leave, I believe

that it is always in your best interest to do so. Sometimes those who are sensitive to spirits may not yet know to what degree they have developed their sensitivity.

Those who are able to see spirit entities also hold the capability to heal spirits who are struggling and caught between two worlds. Using prayer, and visualizing a spirit entity moving away from their current circumstance, is of great help. Also beneficial is repeating a positive visualization that matches the circumstance of an entity whenever you feel their presence. If an entity is an unwelcome visitor, know that their purpose is not to torment you, it is simply that they are lost souls who need direct guidance.

Consider for a moment that we ourselves may have been lost within the experience of the afterlife, in a suspended state for one reason or another. With this in mind, it is important to remember that at all levels, we are connected, and what may appear as a stranger in need, both in life and in the afterlife, may actually be a test of your willingness to help another.

We have to remember that when we feel a visitation of an unpleasant nature, it is really the spirit's discomfort and anger toward themselves that we feel. They are suspended, by choice, in a state of awareness that they are unable to progress through until a personal agenda is met. In other words, until a disincarnate being can gain full understanding that they have crossed over from life, as they knew it in physical form, and are able to let go of any earthly ties that hold them back from their progression, they will continue to reside in a confused state. When they make continued appearances, they are sometimes unknowingly showing their need for spirit rescue. You can think of these types of spirits as children who have lost their way. When we see spirits in this light, we see that we need not be afraid.

If you are able to help a spirit see that they are no longer incarnate, then by all means, help them. If you have no idea how to help them, then it is best to let those who do this kind of work assist the spirit in need. Most often, this is accomplished at a level that we cannot see, but rather feel in the depth of our soul. We are automatically given the tools to help spirit entities find their path back toward evolution. Those who do not respond to the help of their spiritual family, both here and in the afterlife, are sent a rescue worker to guide them from their current lost state of being. Spirit rescues are accomplished with the help of both guides and angels who appear in cases where a disincarnate entity's lost condition no longer serves their spiritual evolution.

Chapter 9
The Presence of Angels

"Be not forgetful to entertain strangers:
for thereby some have entertained angels unawares."
—Hebrews 13:2, *Holy Bible*

The frequency of light that we acquire during consecutive life-times determines our view and understanding of angels. When we have reached the level of consciousness that radiates the same frequency of light that angels emanate, we can then easily feel and see them.

Angels are made of pure light, God's light, which is available to us always, nurturing us in ways often unseen.

Angels have never been in human form, but they can appear in human form, or any form they desire. They are free of all dark molecules within their ethereal vibration and molecular energy pattern, and specialize in every situation possible, including situations that we have pre-created in an afterlife state for the purpose of higher learning and spiritual growth.

Angels, however, do not save us from the daily difficulties of life. Rather, angels appear to us as messengers in life, bringing us a strong light force that helps us to realign our spirits with the source from which we were made.

Is an angel a spirit guide? Angels are not spirit guides but rather messengers who come to you with a powerful guidance when life situations become detrimental to your spirit. At these times, angels appear in many forms—whatever form is acceptable to you—as reminders of your chosen path, especially if you are in a near-death situation. Though death is inviting when you are near death, it may not be your time to go. Part of you will know this, and you will abandon the urge to cross through to the other side.

Another time that we may receive an angel visitation is when our spirit loses its earthly magnetics. In other words, you lose touch with your own physical energy force. This can cause sudden physical distress, of any type, and lead to degenerative physical conditions that tilt the balance of our ethereal beings. Other reasons for losing ourselves include prematurely leaving the earthly plane. This is caused by suicide, murder, or by an accidental and sudden death. This is when your assigned angel, one who is with you through many consecutive deaths, appears and assists you through any sudden crossing phase and the transition into the afterlife.

Angels appear when a great imbalance is about to occur to assure you in the most magnificent way that you are indeed crossing over to a wonderful place that is more akin to home than your current imagination could ever conceive.

Spirit guides are advanced soul entities who, by agreement, are assigned to you and remain with you through consecutive lifetimes. It is not difficult or uncommon to meet your current guide through past-life memory recall. If you are able to look back through your past-life memories (and in my opinion, this is best done only with the intention to heal), you will meet your spirit guide who has helped you cross over lifetime after lifetime.

We have more than one spirit guide who assists us in life. We have, in fact, many. It depends on how much assistance you need, and what your mission in life is, so to speak. This is what determines how many spirit guides are assigned to you throughout your lifetime.

Spirit guides do change as you progress through lifetimes and levels of consciousness. As you gain more wisdom through each consecutive incarnation, you may surpass the duties of a particular guide assigned to you for the experiences you have chosen as necessary for your ascension. When this happens, you are introduced to your next guide, who then takes the place of your prior guide. This type of graduation process is much like that of our schools here on earth. Guides can also be looked upon as our teachers or advisors.

As with angels, guides too have their specialty. Do call upon them when you are in need. They will hear your call and are always within your immediate vicinity.

To hear what your guides in spirit are saying, simply listen to the first voice or mental image that comes to you. This is how your guide speaks.

Angels visually appear according to the belief system of the person who is experiencing the presence of angels. We all have creative minds and view the world from different perspectives. Our belief system and current perspectives greatly influence our perceptions of the world up until the point of our deaths, and immediately following, when we are better able to see with clarity that which we may have never utilized in life, our guides and helpers of our spiritual ascension.

Angels are messengers sent by our creator to deliver to you a message in a way that is both acceptable to you as well as inspiring. Some angels are in human form and exist on a physical, molecular level. That is, their vibrations match that of human vibrations, making them visible to the human eye.

Communication by angels is most often telepathic. This is why many have reported seeing their loved one talking to someone unseen just before they died.

Angels will also appear when you are close to death. Their presence is soft yet certain, and you know instinctively that you are being cared for, and that it is okay to let go of your physical being.

If you are in a situation that is life threatening, angels will appear and take any action necessary to correct what is not in alignment with your pre-planned life in this human incarnation.

I have experienced the presence of angels, as many do, when I was in a car accident in 1990. As it was all happening in slow motion, and my car was smashing up right before my eyes, I saw three angels and a veil. I was in front of the veil and about to go through it, when I was gently pushed back. I heard the words "It is not your time." The next day, though I could hardly move, I had a renewed energy within. I felt the presence of God like I had never felt before I had this near-death experience. I felt reborn.

The veil I saw in this experience was soft and silver, and seemed to be made of a material similar to that of gauze. I knew that though this silver illuminating veil appeared as a curtain, it was actually the fine line that once crossed would allow me to be released from my physical body. I knew that if I crossed this line, I could not come back. I remember this experience to be very inviting and I very much wanted to go, but was not allowed to fully pass through the veil. I only touched it, and as I did, I was swiftly pushed back into my body where I found myself conscious, sitting in the middle of a freeway facing oncoming traffic.

If we have angels, then why do we have spirit guides as well? Angels and guides perform different tasks. Angels deal with helping in a situation that calls for immediate and life-threatening attention, and guides lead us through our everyday life and nudge us toward making decisions that are for our greater good, as well as the greater good of the universe.

You may wonder why some people can speak with their guides on a daily basis while you cannot see yours, let alone talk to them. Well, have no worries. Your guides are well aware of this, and now that you are aware of them, you too can begin to communicate with them.

If you want to hear your guides, you can by quieting your own thoughts and listening within this quiet. What happens for many people is that they ask themselves a question, and then they hear the answer before they themselves have even finished the question. This is your guide speaking to you and offering you suggestions for a course of action.

Both guides and angels can appear in human form and have agreed to this before incarnation. When you meet a guide or angel that is in human form, you may not even recognize them because they come in countless human forms, sometimes that of a child, and even strangers, as we will see in our next story written by Neva.

Angel in the Crowd
by Neva

My mother took me on a cruise last year for sixteen days and there were about two thousand people aboard. At the first port, we had to tender to shore and were asked to meet in the main auditorium. So with my mother, cousin, and his wife, we listened to the instructions given, then we were told that those who were not scheduled for specific tours could leave and go to Deck 4, so we started to go up the aisle to the main door.

I have Post Traumatic Stress Syndrome and tend to panic in large crowds, but I was doing fine and there weren't that many people leaving for Deck 4. Then, all of a sudden, the rest of the people were told to go to Deck 4 as well. The mass-energies seemingly encapsulated me and I began to shake and cry! I heard a voice in my head say, "Get to the rail." So I did and I grabbed the rail firmly and began to look for my mother. Then, a man asked me if I was okay. I said, "No, but I am working on it!" He asked if I was trying to get over there to the lady with white hair and I said yes, having seen her and met my mother's eyes. Then he grabbed my arm and seemingly made an aisle through the throng and firmly took me to my mother and placed my arm in her hand. Then he just disappeared. Poof! I looked for him the rest of the cruise so I could thank him, but never saw him again.

After I returned home, I was talking with my friend and relating the story when all of a sudden the light went off in my head, and I said, "Oh, my, I think he was an angel!" My friend said she got goose bumps when I said that.

I called my mother and asked her if she had seen the man again. My mother said, "What man, honey, I don't remember any man!" Then I began to cry tears of thanksgiving and joy! What a privilege it is to know that we are always watched over and cared for with the highest force of love, by God and his angels.

Author

When we come into the presence of angels, as did Neva, we may not realize at that moment the nature of the help we are receiving. Often, when we later look back on a situation and see that we were indeed in the presence of an angel at a time of great need, we are profoundly touched.

In situations where death is imminent, we may find ourselves talking to angels because we can feel them in our immediate presence. This is what Julie felt when her mother, who was dying, asked her and others in the room if they could hear the hymn "Amazing Grace." Not only are there others who have already crossed over present at our deaths, there is sometimes accompanying music that calms our soul, helping to prepare us for our imminent crossing.

Close to the time of death, Julie felt angels present in her mother's hospital room. The presence of Julie's grandmother and her mother's first baby boy, who had died fifty years before, was felt strongly. This is Julie's experience.

My Mum's Departure from This World
by Julie

Knowing my mum had cancer was hard enough, but living 1,500 kilometers away from her was not easy, as I had my own family to think about and not a lot of money with which to visit frequently.

Once I got the phone call that her time was running out, I was on the plane in a flash, though I wasn't sure if I would even make it. Only God knew she had a week left on this earth.

During that time I, along with my three sisters, did things for my mother I never would have dreamt I had the courage to do. It was almost like going the full cycle; our mum was like the baby and we were the mums!

The day before Mum died, we had bathed her and washed her hair at her request. When helping her back to bed, I felt her bones collapse under my arms, so I knew time was running out. My husband and kids were on their way by car.

Once Mum was comfortable, she just lay there with a smile on her face asking if we could hear the music. We all knew she was the only one hearing the hymn "Amazing Grace" and were happy for her.

The shivers came over me as I felt the angels in the room. They were huge and powerful and all I could think about was their power, a power and strength that had come to carry this frail little woman to meet her God. I adamantly walked to the door and pleaded with the angels to come back tomorrow so that my husband and kids could get the chance to say good-bye. It sounds rather brash now, but I told them they could have her forever, and I begged for God to let my family visit my mum and to have our prayers answered now. For months now, we had prayed every night that we would get to say good-bye. Mum went to sleep and I felt that my prayers had been answered.

The next afternoon, my family arrived. Any strength Mum had left came in the form of a huge smile that lit up her face when they arrived. I will never forget it.

The following morning at 2 a.m., we woke to spend what would be the last three hours with our mum. In the last half hour of my mum's life, she saw her own mum and her first baby boy who had died almost fifty years ago, when he was three days old.

I sat with my mum and said the Rosary (I am no longer involved in the Catholic Church, but my mum was very faithful to it). As I said the "Our Father" and "Hail Mary" and waited for her last breath, I remember asking her a silly question. "Can't you breathe, Mum?" and when she shook her head no, I said, "Do you want to?" She nodded yes, and with that, she died. It just shows the strength of the human spirit, the will to live, never giving up.

Author

Naturally, it is sometimes difficult to recognize the final moment of death as a wonderful and well-planned release, not only for those of us who may fear death and do not want to let go, but also for friends and family members who may be present at the time of your death.

Moments before dying, you will see that all pain is lifted from the physical body. We can try to hang on until the very last second, but these attempts will be in vain. Light that is so undeniably the light of our Creator will appear, and you will willingly let go of any previous conceptions you held in life, allowing yourself to move from your physical body.

Immediately before death, we often release ourselves from the notion that we cease to exist once we exit our bodies, because visitations before our deaths help us to realize this. As well, those who are present during our crossing often change their point of view concerning death, especially after experiencing angel and spirit visitations, which are most always felt strongly in the presence of a death.

During the final moments before we die, we will see that death requires crossing a symbolic bridge; a bridge that once crossed no longer requires a physical form. Our energy will instantly become renewed, and we again remember our light bodies, our substance, which is seen with greater clarity once we return to the afterlife, a place where we no longer require anything physical.

Chapter 10

The Dynamics of Healing

"Vision is the art of seeing the invisible."
—*Jonathan Swift*

Healing visitations have had an impact on the health of individuals since time began. The diversity of healing visitations is unlimited, both in appearance and in strength. In other words, there is no limit to healing. The only thing that limits anyone in any particular area of healing is the belief that healing comes from somewhere other than themselves.

Healing is often attributed to higher sources outside ourselves, or to those people who hold seemingly out-of-the-ordinary or extraordinary gifts. As it happens, it is not the will of others that make a healing occur, it is your own will that prompts healing within.

When we receive healing assistance, in any form, what is really happening is that we are allowing another to help us to reconnect with our own innate ability to heal ourselves.

If you have ever had a spirit visitation or intuitively think that you may have, I feel certain that you were aware at the time that you were witnessing a special event. These healing occurrences—visitations that heal—are of great comfort, and also serve as a reminder that your innate healing abilities are accessible to you always.

Healers work in many different ways. Knowing this, we can then say that one healing method is not better than another. What makes a particular healing method useful is that you respond to it in a life-giving and uplifting way. The most useful healing method is a method that returns you to your center, and consciously calls your spirit back to itself.

When we feel out of balance, we have temporarily lost a part of our spirit. What we want to do when we realize this has happened is to call that part of our spirit, once we have determined where it has gone, back to our present time and being. Sometimes this includes calling our spirit back from previous lifetimes. In this sense, we experience healing visitations both from and for ourselves in the same instant.

Many people have experienced meeting others we have known from previous lifetimes and immediately felt a deep connection and longing to return to that previous time, especially if it was a time of great love. In order to preserve the same feelings, people often try to re-create the same experience now, in their current life, that they remember from a previous lifetime. The misconception here is that what you have already experienced has already happened. It is a recollection of the past. Therefore, you have to ask, "Are you now in the present time, or are you allowing your spirit to wander from the present? If so, then why?"

If this situation resembles your present circumstances in life, perhaps your energy is being sacrificed by dwelling in the past, when it may better serve you to keep your attention in the present time. This is one reason that you can become spiritually exhausted. If you exert energy for reasons that have nothing to do with your current situation and life circumstances, you are not serving your present needs.

If we have in fact escaped the present by spending a lot of time in our past, when we decide to reconnect to ourselves in the present time, we may notice that we have created blocked or stagnated energy to work through.

How can we move through blocked energy that may be pre-venting us from complete healing and health? To identify any part of yourself that may be blocked, any part of you that is pre-venting you from living fully, you can simply sit with yourself and note the first three memories that come to you when you ask yourself the question, "What is preventing me from living fully?" When you receive the answers to what is preventing you from living fully, then ask, "What is it I am to do now?" As hard as it may be to believe, answers will come to you. This is your higher guidance speaking. Often answers may come to you be-fore you even finish asking your question. You may not like the answers that you hear, as they may take great effort and change on your part. Nevertheless, the answers will come. Continue to repeat this exercise until you no longer receive anything that is causing you imbalance.

Healing, at any level, is a responsibility. Healing is the re-sponsibility not only to yourself, but to everyone. When you come to a point in your life where you discover something has got to change, most likely this will be an opportunity for you to take the next step on your chosen path to becoming free from anything that restricts or limits you in any way. You may won-der, "How this going to happen?" when you feel so alone. The key is to recognize that you are not alone in this process. An invisible army, which works twenty-four hours a day in honor of your evolution, surrounds you. So, whenever you are ready, know you have many helpers standing by.

When you make the decision to change your current condi-tioning as well as any thoughts that create your conditioning, parts of your old self will fall away, making room for the con-scious part of you that has been waiting to express itself. To do this, we have to allow for change.

When you seek to change your life, it is important to be aware of, and remove, any trapped or seemingly impaired en-ergy within your physical body. This is so you can once again begin to freely create your life as you would like it to be. For those of you who just said in your mind, "But I am not a creative person," know that all that is preventing you from your creations is simply blocked energy. When you consciously work on removing what is blocking your energy from moving freely throughout your being, you will be able to create with ease, making not only what you have always dreamed of for your own life, but also that which you never knew you were capable of creating.

When you have had the experience of a supernatural healing or a healing visitation, it becomes outstanding and you want to tell everyone about it, especially if it happened in a church environment where holy experiences are most assuredly accepted. Today, we call these experiences "miracles."

If you have experienced a healing that includes visual spirit entities, and it does not happen in a church, often anything of a paranormal healing nature—that which cannot be explained by science—is looked upon by others with raised eyebrows and speculation. Not only can this reaction leave you alone in your healing experience, it often leaves you without direction or reference material that can help you to understand the dynamics of healings of a paranormal nature.

Healing visitations offer comfort in showing you that someone you loved, and still love, is able to communicate with you even after death. Healing visitations also help to lessen our grief and bring a new perspective on healing, especially at times when we thought it might not be possible for us to heal.

Grief comes from our inability to understand that death is a false impression and perception when death is associated with an end. Grief, a deep mental anguish, arises from the inability to conceptualize that we are of one spirit, and are never separated, even by death.

If we are more aware and alive after our death, and are able to see our past lives and make future lifetime decisions from a perspective that is most beneficial to our evolutional growth, then it seems to follow that when we die, what is actually happening is that we are being birthed back to the place from which we came.

Once we are aware that we do exist beyond our physical being, we become more open to communication with spirit energies that reside beyond our physical five senses (hearing, touch, smell, taste, and sight) and begin to recognize that we are intuitive and boundless.

Those who have not developed the ability to communicate beyond five senses will often seek the counsel of a medium. Many people seek mediums and pay enormous amounts of money, only to find out something they could have learned on their own if they only knew that all information, and everything they needed for healing, already exists within them. By remembering this, and in some cases reuniting with our sixth sense, we are able to realign with unseen forces and guides who help us to discover the healing capabilities that are possible and always available to us.

Learning to get back in touch with the part of yourself where you learn to believe in your own instincts is in part learning to heal. In other words, it is important to be able to listen for the guiding voice that speaks to you anytime you are seeking answers that both support you in every way and also work to heal your life to the fullest capacity possible. This means reaching a point in your life where you feel that you are in complete and total balance—balance not only in your everyday activities, but also in your relationship to the part of yourself that only desires to heal.

When we feel both balanced and healed up to this present moment, it is then that light is able to pass through us without obstruction. It is then that we can resume creating our lives from a place where we have learned to become sensitive to higher energies, energies that not only help to balance the body in all ways, but also to heal those parts of ourselves that are obstructing the movement of our own life force. Once we remember the well of life force available to us now, we will remember the part of ourselves that automatically heals. Once we remember, healing naturally resumes.

Chapter 11
Spontaneous Memories of Children's Past Lives

"The most promising evidence bearing on
reincarnation seems to come from the spontaneous
cases, especially among children."
—*Dr. Ian Stevenson*

Spontaneous past-life memories recalled by children are both surprising and often astonishing. What makes what children have to say so interesting regarding past lives? Primarily, it is that children are able to recall, and recite in detail, information from time periods that they have seemingly not experienced. What a child says, speaking candidly about their past-life memories, can be substantiated by physical evidence that the child, on no account, could have known about. This evidence includes factual documentation such as the name the child mentions they had in a past lifetime, places that are spontaneously recognized (such as previously unknown towns or cities where the child can tell you what is around the corner), and recognition of family members both in person and in photos they may have never seen before.

The following story, about a little girl who returns to her family, helps us to recognize that it is possible for family members to leave this physical world and return to us again within our same lifetime. Not only do our children return to us, they can tell us what they were doing while they were in-between incarnations, and who they were with.

He Watches Over Me
by Janet

My grandfather passed away on the same day that I had an emergency C-section to try to save one of my twin babies. The estimated time of death for that little girl and my grandfather was the same hour on the same day!

Before my granddad passed away, he told me and a cousin of mine (for verification, perhaps) that in a year and a week, my baby twin that was going with him would be born back to me. One year and a week later, I had a baby girl. A coincidence? You decide.

Years later, my daughter was in preschool and began to talk about a man with white hair. Could it be? She told me about how he would push her on a swing and read stories. Then she told me something about when I was a little girl that only my granddad would have known! My daughter had never seen a picture of her granddad, so I got one and put it in with a bunch of others. Shortly thereafter, my daughter picked it out and said, "This is the man with the white hair, Mommy!" About all I could do was to take a deep breath and say, "Yes, dear, it is! He is your great granddad," to which she replied, "I know, he watches over me."

Author
We can tell when a child is speaking of a past life because their demure changes as well as their vocabulary and tempo of speech. It is as if they are reliving the visual aspects of a past life, seeing clearly what is before them as they speak of a time when they were not yet born.

The spontaneous memories of children's past lives help us to see that our children, in this present day, are more aware in consciousness than we may recognize. We now see that children who speak of past lifetimes are bringing forth a knowledge and wisdom that can help us all to better understand the dynamics of reincarnation and children who remember their past lives.

In the following story, Scott, a three-year-old boy, remembers his past lifetime with his grandmother in this life, whom Scott says was his older sister at that previous time, and a man named Lunkins. Scott depicts, in detail, a time when he lived on a farm with Lunkins, whom Scott recalls to be his grandfather sometime back when Abraham Lincoln was president.

Lunkins
Anonymous

When my grandson Scott was three years old, he began to talk a lot about his grandfather, whom he says was named Lunkins. I asked him once if we know anyone named Lunkins now, and he told me no, that Lunkins does not really want to come back for a while. He talked about how he misses him sometimes.

According to Scott, we lived on a farm when they used mules and plows. Scott says Lunkins came to America from Germany. I didn't even know Scott knew of a place called Germany. He talks about transportation being wooden cars that horses pulled, but Lunkins was too poor to have horses, so he had mules.

Scott will ask me if I remember when all we had to drink back then was milk or water. He also said that sometimes Lunkins had coffee, but it was "yucky."

He seems to have really cared about this Lunkins character, since that is mostly what he talks about. Lately he has been asking me to take him to Lunkins's grave. I told him I didn't know where it was.

Scott has so many stories that it is hard to tell them all. But he doesn't tell them like stories. It is more like things we did just the other day. He has recently mentioned that I was his older sister.

I have never known anyone by the name of Lunkins. I have asked Scott if his dad or any of my other children were with us at that time, and he says no. Sometimes I will talk along with him on some of it because he acts as if he just cannot believe I don't remember. As for the time period, all I have gotten is the type of transportation used, and that our toys were made of straw. Scott talks as though it was a very happy time.

Once Scott was sitting on my lap, looking at my face, and he asked me if I was going to get wrinkly like Lunkins did when he got old. That's when I asked him how Lunkins died, and he said, "He got real sick and died."

Scott talks about Lunkins having arthritis a lot. In addition, he mentions how Lunkins did not get along with one of his neighbors. He says Lunkins was always happy until he was angry with his neighbor. Nevertheless, he usually laughs about Lunkins arguing with his neighbor. He also talks about something Lunkins's wife would fix when anyone would get sick that must have tasted very bad. He says, "It looked kind of like a hamburger but had a lot of different things in it to make you better." Another strange thing Scott has said is that he has always been around me, but was waiting for the right time to be with me.

Long before Scott came into my life, I kept having the same dream over and over about a white-headed little boy that I was just crazy about. In the dream, he was my little boy, but also he wasn't. When I would wake up, I could not understand how this child could be my child, but not my child. In the dream, I was always fighting for custody of him and was afraid of losing him. I remember telling my friends that I didn't know why I kept having that dream, because my kids were all teenagers, and I knew I wouldn't be fighting for them. They were almost grown.

Scott's mother abandoned him when he was six months old, and a year later, came back to get him. Scott didn't even know who she was, so I found myself in court for a custody hearing. The judge immediately gave custody to me. I have since been raising the most adorable little white-headed boy that isn't my child, but my grandchild.

When Scott started kindergarten, for a while he didn't mention Lunkins. Though since the presidential campaign, Scott has been talking about how Lunkins said Abraham Lincoln was the best president we ever had. I don't know where he heard that Abraham Lincoln was the best president we ever had. I don't even know where he heard about Abraham Lincoln! I do know they have not studied about him in school yet. When I asked him where he had heard of him, he told me Lunkins used to talk about him. Scott also said, "Lunkins fought in that war that was going on when Abraham Lincoln was president."

Author

Scott's recollection of a past life at age three is a classic example of a child's past-life memory. As we can see from Scott's memories, his concepts and vocabulary are more advanced than those of a three-year-old child. Scott mentions items in his past life such as toys (which at the time, were made of straw), coffee and its taste, the types of animals used for plowing fields, geographical locations such as America and Germany, and that Abraham Lincoln was president during that lifetime. These are all explicit examples of the knowledge of a past life that are difficult to refute.

When children effortlessly discuss their past lives with us and include details that are beyond their age-appropriate and historical understanding, it can be shocking and sometimes uncomfortable for the parents, who often do not know how to respond. This forces us, as caretakers and parents, to take a new look at the way we perceive our world, the afterlife, and reincarnation. Often we will discover that it is our own children who have been with us before in a previous lifetime, and with them, they bring to this current life the history of our own past lives.

When we explore the past-life memories of our children, we often find we are included in their recollections. This confirms, beyond a doubt, that we can and do reincarnate back into the same families, but often with interchanging roles.

Tina's story about her daughter is among one of the most fascinating accounts of a child's past-life memory. Tina's daughter, at age four, remembers a time when the roles were reversed, and Tina's daughter was her mother in a previous lifetime.

Old Soul
by Tina

I have an amazing four-year-old. Most children are amazing, but I have come to realize that she is an old soul. You can feel and see it in her presence.

One day while sitting in the kitchen, my daughter told me I was her daughter, her father was her son, and our son was her son as well. She also said that her cousin was her son, and that she had another daughter. I asked her how many children she had, and she said five. She sat and continued talking about the things we did and was so comfortable about it that I just let her talk. I truly believed her. She is very well versed and always asks me if I remember when? Most of the time, I have to say that I don't. It really upsets her when I tell her that.

Author
It is a very common reaction for children to become upset when they sense that you may not completely understand their past-

life experiences. The difficulty for both parents and caregivers alike is that learning to deal successfully with the past-life memories of children is not something that has been a part of the standard practice in child rearing.

If you are a parent or caregiver who finds you are listening to a child who depicts another life and time in detail, as Tina's daughter did, you are not alone. Today, more and more children are born with a capacity that far surpasses the normal capabilities we are used to experiencing with children. These children are termed the New or Indigo children.

It is said that Indigo children have appeared roughly within the last thirty-five years, but I would hesitate to make such a marked statement because if we are just now learning to understand and identify with their extraordinary gifts, how can we possibly tell, with certainty, how long they have been incarnating to our planet?

Indigo children bring a healing energy that resonates at higher frequencies, helping us to align our energies to their highest possible potential. The most pronounced capability in Indigo children is the ability to access the natural channels and finite energies that surround us. By bringing this energy into our presence, Indigo children assist in the preparations necessary for the ascension of the whole of humanity. This is the principal purpose of Indigo children.

Indigo children are born with a changing DNA makeup that protects them from serious human illnesses that are currently circulating our planet. This enables them to continue with the work they came here to do without physical interference. These children are natural healers and are essentially immune to all diseases. They can read your mind, and have an intellectual capacity that far exceeds that of an adult.

Indigo children often display behavior that is overconfident because, in fact, they are confident and are able to explain concepts that adults can only begin to comprehend. In addition,

they do not respond well to authority and feel that the imple-
mentation of discipline is discourteous, both to them and to
their own innate wisdom.

Indigo children often have difficulty with standard schooling
because it does not meet the needs of these fully-aware children, who become increasingly bored and eventually frustrated. Their frustration stems from always seeing a better way
to do things at home, in school, and in other social environ-
ments. In addition, Indigo children often desire to accomplish
tasks that are far advanced for their age. This can create a constant battle of the minds for both children and parents alike if
parents are not aware of their child's gifts, and mistake them for
behavioral problems, namely Attention Deficit Disorder
(ADD).

Indigo children need special care and attention as well as
protection from those who misinterpret their advanced concepts and label them fictitious. This is not only discouraging, it
is harmful to their inner light, which they have come to share
openly.

It is up to each of us to protect all children from anything that
may hinder their spiritual growth. This includes protection
from our own beliefs and disbeliefs, which should never be
placed in the minds of children who characteristically show an
interest in their own personal beliefs and ideas at a young age.

If you feel you cannot possibly begin to understand the idea
that a child can have a consciousness that is elevated to the
point where they can see at multiple dimensions, consider the
circumstances. Maybe you have a very aware child for a specific
reason. Perhaps they are your teachers, and have come to you
for the very first time. Perhaps they are a deceased relative, who
has reincarnated to be with you in your current lifetime. Whatever the reason that you discover, and you eventually will,
know that these enlightened children, including those who remember past lives, chose you as their caregiver, and that they

would not have made this choice if you were not spiritually qualified. Once we honor the fact that our children choose us as parents and caregivers, then we can allow ourselves to be open to the new ideas and teachings brought forth by them.

The memories of children's past lives teach us that the possibility that we return to this earth and live again is great. They also teach us that our children's experiences are not limited to age, and that they will effortlessly discuss previous lifetimes with us if we are sincere in our attempt to understand our children and their past lives.

Chapter 12

Reunions from Previous Lifetimes

"Whenever I am born in every life to come, may I
meet again my Guardian Angel of this life!
Speaking and understanding the moment I am born,
may I . . . remember my former lives!"
—*The Tibetan Book of the Dead*

Throughout your many consecutive incarnations, the same
spiritual family members will continue to meet you. You will
know them when you meet them because you will instantly feel
a great familiarity with one another. You may not understand
why, or know what it is about a particular person that feels so
familiar; it is just something about them that reignites a lifetime
bond the instant that you meet. A picture of another moment in
time may come to mind, and may include the person whom you
have just met. Many do not even think that an instant recollection could actually be part of a past-life memory recall. However, when you learn to recognize the feelings that go along
with the memories of a past life, you will immediately feel at
home, and completely comfortable with the person with whom
you are sharing your experience.

The Reverend J. L. writes about the past-life recollection she
had after she made an appointment with a new doctor. Upon
her arrival, she found that she knew the doctor from a previous lifetime. Not only did Rev. J. L. recognize the doctor, he
also recognized her as well. This is a classic example of a past-

life recollection. We know it to be a true recollection, because two people recognize the same memory simultaneously.

The Appointment
by Rev. J. L.

Back in the mid-1980s, I went to a doctor and had a strange feeling that I knew him from before . . . then it hit me! It was a past life I was remembering, and not only did I recognize him, he recognized me! We had a rather pleasant discussion, although not quite of the average kind! It is not every day that you meet someone face-to-face that you have shared a past life with, and both admit to it.

Author

To meet a person and recognize that you have shared a past together is one of the rarer experiences two people can have. As one progresses spiritually in consciousness, experiences of recognizing others as familiar increase. Once we begin to experience this increase in familiarity, we move into a new understanding of our relationship to others. We see that people are not strangers unless we make them so.

When we do not allow others into our lives, especially for superficial reasons, we may indeed be blinded to someone who has been a close relation to us in a past lifetime. As each of us grows in consciousness, separation falls away and we are better able to recognize a familiarity within one another that we often can associate with a past lifetime.

The concept that we are interconnected to another person in any way is sometimes a difficult concept to grasp. With such a diversity of people in the world, on occasion we may have a difficult time both relating to and associating with others. However, when we can understand that reaction to diversity of any kind is based solely on our perceptions, which may alter at any given moment, then we can better understand how we are connected to another, if we recognize that our perceptions of others may indeed on occasion be false perceptions.

What happens when you remember past lives is that you are recognizing yourself (your former self from a past life) in another person, who holds the energy of your memories, and you, theirs.

We create and attract our spiritual and physical family members according to the energy resonance we carry both here and in the afterlife. Sometimes even though the desire to be with someone again whom you loved in a past lifetime may be great, it does not necessarily mean that you will both incarnate in human form at the same time again. Meeting again depends on many factors, namely that both parties continue to reside at the same energy frequency (both while incarnated, and in an out-of-body state), and have planned for future physical incarnations together.

Remembering past lives is experienced by both children and adults alike. As our consciousness continues to expand, we are better able to remember our past-life experiences that have been happening since the beginning of our creation.

In the following past-life experience, we shall see how two people, Debbie and her husband in a past life, can plan to meet in a future lifetime. We also recognize that Debbie is one of many thousands of people who can remember one of her past lifetimes, in detail, as being part of the Lost Civilization of Atlantis, where she was named Kara. In that life, she knew a man, Seji, who was her late husband in this lifetime. We shall see through Debbie's detailed recollection of her Atlantean life that her days were limited, and that she indeed experienced the last days of Atlantis.

Atlantis
by Debbie

In the last lifetime I experienced in Atlantis, I was a female named Kara. Kara was quite petite with long blond hair. She also wore very straight dresses to her ankles, and flat shoes. She had a boyfriend named Seji (my late husband in this life).

During this lifetime on Atlantis, the population was in serious trouble and the end was near. A faction called the Sons of Belial had taken control of the crystal energy power and was using it for their own benefit. They were controlling a large segment of the population, using mind control, and turning people into slaves to answer to the Belial's whims and fancies. They were an evil group opposing the Sons of the Law of One.

In each temple on Atlantis was a large crystal that provided energy. To have control of these crystals meant that you had control over the people as well as the knowledge to utilize the crystal energy.

Seji had been chosen to take artifacts from Atlantis, by boat, to Egypt, where they were to be kept safe inside the Great Pyramid. These pyramids were a common form on Atlantis, as they are throughout the universe on other inhabited planets. Things had deteriorated so badly with the Belial group that the Law of One knew destruction was at hand. It became mandatory to remove many things from Atlantis for safekeeping and to make sure the history of the land was not totally lost when the destruction came. Special chambers had been built beneath the pyramid especially for this purpose.

Kara used many different crystals. It was common practice on Atlantis to utilize these energies on a personal basis. She used two beautifully polished, clear crystals by holding them to her temples with the pointed end out. This was to purify the mind, as the negative energies and thoughts would leave through the points. She used another against one temple to enhance her telepathic abilities. She also had a wonderful amethyst crystal in the shape of a pyramid, but all the corners were rounded off, including the top peak. It was about two inches in diameter. She would place the pointed end to her forehead and this was to receive spiritual wisdom.

One day, Seji left on a mandatory mission, and Kara was left behind. Shortly after Seji left, Kara was walking in a canyon and an earthquake started. Kara felt the earth begin to give way under her feet and tried to climb out, but the ground opened up, and took her into the abyss. This was the end of Atlantis.

Author

Those who have previously lived on Atlantis are advanced both in soul age and in their innate ability to heal others. They have natural wisdom with reference to crystals, and the expertise to use them.

Once you experience the power of an elevated civilization such as Atlantis, it becomes part of your soul memory at a molecular level. This makes remembering and connecting with others who have experienced the same civilization with you effortless.

Edgar Cayce, an ordinary man with remarkable psychic talents, spoke about Atlantis in detail, frequently referring to previous lives on Atlantis while reading other people's past lifetimes during a twenty-year period of active Cayce readings, from 1923 to 1944. Today, copies of over fourteen thousand of Edgar Cayce's readings, as well as the follow-up reports received from the individuals who had asked for the readings, are available to the public at the Association for Research and Enlightenment (A.R.E.) founded by Edgar Cayce in Virginia Beach, Virginia, in 1931.

Many things can separate us from those who we love—above all, death. The death of another can cause great devastation at the soul level, sometimes so much so that we become blinded to the truth that can help to release us from our devastation, the truth that death is only a transformation.

When we can learn to understand that we can never be separated, even by death, we can better understand that those who appear as if they have deceased are only gone in a physical form. After death, we can continue relationships with those we knew in life once we understand that we are able to communicate at many other different levels, both in life and in death. The ability to make this communication depends on your awareness that the possibility to do so exists. In the following story, Richard shares with us a conversation he had with his former wife from a past lifetime, Theodora, whom he had known approximately two thousand years ago. What makes Richard's story distinctive is that he brings forth a perspective on life, Theodora's perspective, from another dimension.

Theodora's Vaster Perspective
by Richard

I've been communicating for a while now with someone in spirit during out-of-body experiences, whom I'm pretty close with at the soul level. She's another scholarly type, as I am. I call her by a nickname, Theo, short for Theodora. I think she passed over to the spirit realm sometime in the late 1990s, in an auto wreck due to the drunk driving of someone else. I think she was in her late teens or early twenties when this happened, and I know that she had a baby boy. She has told me that we knew each other in Alexandria, Egypt, sometime about two thousand years ago, and that we were also husband and wife as Native Americans when the Europeans came to North America, among many other lifetimes of knowing each other. I recently asked her, "What surprises you the most when you review your last lifetime?" and she shared a sequence of symbolic images with me. I will interpret them as best I can.

She viewed her two spirit guides immediately after passing over as being good witches, kind of like Glenda, the good witch, in *The Wizard of Oz*.

She wondered at first why some people were so "muddy" energetically on the lower levels of the astral plane, and why they didn't seem to really notice it or even care, for that matter.

She felt very angry at first when she realized how exposed all of her thoughts and actions had been during her life to those in the spirit realm, unbeknownst to her.

It surprised her to realize how most people she had known during her life were effectively dead due to being stuck in the daily routine of their job, and how few people in the physical world are truly alive. She could see where she was in the process of becoming deadened in the same way when she passed over.

It surprised her how blind most people in the physical world are without even realizing it, and how distorted their view of reality and of each other is.

She felt that she and other people she knew spent too much time watching TV, and, it surprised her to realize that she was actually being held accountable for everything that she had said and done during her life.

Author

Theodora, and her continuing support to Richard, offers many helpful insights with regard to her view and thoughts concerning her most recent lifetime here on earth. She mentions the many things she did not see while she was living, and found that when she died, her ethereal vision of her physical life, and that of others, became clear.

The insights Theodora brings from the afterlife are profound. It is my greatest hope that they are also of inspiration and benefit to you, especially the main message from Theodora, which is that you will be held accountable for everything that you have ever said or done during your lifetime.

Chapter 13
Past Lives and Healing

"Every incarnation that we remember
must increase our comprehension of
ourselves as who we are."
—*Aleister Crowley*

When we remember our past lives, we often tend to recall the manner in which we died, and even that of another's death. This is because we are frequently able to see whole time-periods associated with a past-life memory, and this includes the memories that have touched us deeply.

The benefit of remembering a past life is that it brings us in touch with our innate gravitation toward healing. We begin to allow ourselves to move through any obstacles that may temporarily be preventing us from advancing in this lifetime.

Many people continuously live with unexplained fears of the seemingly silliest things, and without explanation. However, when we look at our fears from the perspective that their origin may come from a previous lifetime, our perception begins to change, and we may see that perhaps there is a good reason for any existing fears we may experience in our current lives. Often, examining fears that cannot be explained medically or otherwise can bring us to the forefront of perceptible blocks within our physical and emotional state of being.

In order to maintain the highest level of balance within our mind, body, and spirit, it is important to eliminate all fear in totality. Fear not only blocks self-perpetuating healing energy, it can also prevent you from moving ahead on your evolutional journey.

Fears and physical ailments that exist in our human body but are without psychological or physiological medical cause can often be traced to memories carried over from previous incarnations. These fears and ailments appear in the body in the form of petrified energy, and can easily be detected by someone who is able to read the energy within the circulatory system of human beings. For those who can do this, it is as easy for them to see as rocks on a sandy beach. If we look at sand as moving energy molecules in the tide, and rocks as trapped energy—molecules grouped together, forming a slower-moving mass that energy cannot easily pass through—then we can better visualize trapped energy within our own energy field and physical form.

To maximize the energy flow within our human body, any masses or trapped energy molecules that are blocking us in any way must be released. Then we can again begin to live fully.

Once we address what it is that prevents us from living fully, that is, anything that no longer serves our higher good, we can eliminate it from our lives, and progressively raise our conscious state in bodily form.

In order to heal any experience, we have to choose to bring ourselves back from our past to the present moment, where we now live. We then must realize that all experiences we have had in the past have already served their purpose and are no longer of life-giving value. You will know the difference between life-giving or life-taking experiences when you stop to ask yourself if any particular experience is depleting you or enhancing your present experience.

Past-life healing, helping someone to return to the present time, is a method that is now being acknowledged as a viable method of healing. Today, more and more medical practitioners are seeing that when traditional diagnosis renders no result, returning to previous lifetimes can be beneficial. Often, a patient's past lives are read, with permission, by a person who is capable of detecting the cause of any residing ailment within the physical body that has nothing to do with this current lifetime.

Lifetime readings are done by looking into another person's past lives and identifying any places where the energy movement within that person is lessened, or at a standstill. The areas of slower molecular movement are then read as a book of that person's experiences, and the information is then brought forth to them. This type of healing is referred to as *long-distance* or *remote healing*, and can be done over great distances, whereby the healer uses his or her ability to look at another's past lives.

Healings often occur naturally after information concerning a past life is brought forth. Past-life memories can happen spontaneously, or can be purposefully looked at with the assistance of someone who is qualified to do past-life readings. When we can look at our past from the present perspective and realize that all past-life experiences have already been experienced, we can then move forward.

In order to have the clearest possible perspectives in life, you must remain in this current life at all times. When you can achieve this, you will no longer have the time, energy, or desire to allow any past experience to remove you from the present, nor will you allow any past lifetime memories to affect your present state of well-being.

You may wonder, "How is it possible to read another person's past lives?" Past, present, and future are all the same, and this is why those who understand this concept are able to read the past lives of others. I call this *clear viewing*.

Clear viewing is as simple as reading a book or watching a movie on a screen. Flashes of life—past, present, and future— come streaming toward you, allowing you to see another person's past lives as well as their current and future ones. Those who have developed this ability are often in direct contact with their guides in spirit.

It is important, on each of our paths, that we always forgive ourselves for any wrongs we may identify when we look at our previous lifetimes. The lessons of forgiveness are easily understood when we realize and know inside that those who have crossed over instantly see and know all errors that may have gone unrealized in this life. When we can clearly understand this concept, that all wrongs are immediately known and forgiven when we die, we can then better understand that it is no longer necessary or beneficial to harbor resentment of any kind that has long been forgiven by all heavenly beings.

Remembering our past lives helps us to become conscious of the present time, and allows us to see that we do not die, and will continue to live repeatedly, creating scenarios for our higher evolutional development.

Chapter 14

Healings of a Paranormal Nature

"There are only two ways to live your life. One is as
though nothing is a miracle. The other is as though
everything is a miracle."
—*Albert Einstein*

Healing offers us the opportunity to become at one with our
higher states of awareness. Sometimes we may get glimpses of
these higher states, and when we do, it is truly a gift.

A higher state of awareness is simply that of what you already are, recognized. It is the wisdom that has been with you
always.

When we are born, we can carry over into this life a part of a
past-life experience that may have been particularly painful,
and continues to burden us in our lives today. All painful experiences, if not acknowledged, settle somewhere in your physical
body, and remain there until you are ready to address why they
are there in the first place.

When we can begin healing any situation by seeing ourselves
as we were at the beginning of our existence, with the ability to
create anything that we desire, we can then see that we are well
equipped, and always have been, to handle any situation that is
before us now, or that is presented to us in the future. Within
any situation, we have alternatives, and healing greatly depends on your personal choice in any matter before you.

Healings occur daily, in every corner of the world, and are frequently underestimated and misunderstood because some of the methods used for healing are not visually perceptible and are carried out on faith.

The act of healing is like cultivating a seed. Once planted in the subconscious, it has no choice but to flourish and grow. This is how you heal. You heal by first wanting to, and then by allowing the natural innate desire to heal within, to work within you. Once the thought and decision to heal has been made, it is as if you have just watered, for the first time, the new seeds of your decision. As the way of nature goes, once planted, a seed has no other alternative but to grow.

In 1958, John observed a miracle, a spontaneous healing of his roommate's hand. His college roommate was suffering from a very rare tumor in his right hand, and needed surgery as soon as possible. The prospect of many hours of surgery was the only alternative, except for prayer, so John's roommate began to pray. His prayers were so loud that at times John would have to leave their shared room. On a Sunday morning after many days of praying, John's roommate woke up to find that the tumor was gone. All that was left was a hole in his hand where the tumor had been.

As we shall see in the following story, the power of prayer carries a strength that is beyond measure.

A Spontaneous Healing
by John

I went to college in New Mexico in 1958. My roommate for the second semester of my freshman year was both a lay Baptist minister and an engineering student. One day, he noticed a slight bump on his right hand. He ignored it for a while and the bump grew larger and larger, until it almost had the characteristic of being the head of a large spike under the skin.

He went to see the college doctor, who ran a couple of quick tests and referred him to a doctor in El Paso, where he soon went. There, he received terrible news. His hand was carefully examined and then X-rayed. The doctor there told him that he had a tumor that was almost like bone in its toughness. It was growing and already had the shape of an octopus, where the ends of the tentacles were constantly pushing out and expanding. Unless surgical intervention was taken, the tumor would continue to grow and expand and eventually would wreck his entire hand. The only choice was to have it cut out, but that was in itself a very harsh prospect. He would have to undergo surgery that might last for ten to twenty hours, where his hand would be carefully taken apart and then the tumor "sawed" apart, piece by piece, and extreme care would have to be taken to ensure that no nerve was damaged during the process.

He began to pray and pray and at times, his prayers were almost too loud, and I would have to leave the room that we shared in college.

Then one Sunday morning, I was awakened by his screams. "It's gone, it's gone!" he repeatedly yelled over and over again. I got up and sure enough, where there had been a tumor about half an inch in diameter, there was a hole that one could put one's finger through to the other side, though of course, the skin was still there on both sides of the hole. It was truly a miracle!

Author

When a person experiences a spontaneous healing, it often becomes necessary to reevaluate his or her conscious understanding of life. He or she must encompass a new perspective toward experiences that are scientifically unexplainable, such as the overnight disappearance of a rare tumor.

We have seen through John's descriptions that healings of a paranormal nature do exist, and that the possibility of using prayer to heal oneself, and having it actually work, is immense. Anyone who experiences extraordinary healings, such as that depicted with John's roommate, knows that it not only changes your perspective on life forever, it offers hope where before there was thought to be none.

Healings come from the source of our creator, who always hears our prayers, and continually heals and nurtures each of us on a moment-to-moment basis. When we understand that we are never alone in this world, we can feel confident in knowing that nothing in our life ever goes unnoticed. If we feel hopeless, we must remember that there are arms to catch us, should we fall.

Johnson lost someone he deeply valued and made the decision, out of desperation and deep sorrow, to take his own life by hanging. During his continued efforts to tie a knot in a rope, he found that his own hands were working against his will. As we shall see, Johnson felt both a presence and a great white light in the room with him that communicated to him without words and saved him from death.

Saved by the Hands of God
by Johnson

Eighteen years ago, I tried to commit suicide. I had lost someone I deeply valued and I was devastated. I waited for my parents to leave for work, then took a rope and tied it to the ceiling fan to hang myself. I was then horrified to see my own hands working against my will and opening the knot and it was then that I felt the presence of someone else in the room. I became more determined and again tried to hang myself, and again and again the same thing happened. It felt so weird, but I gritted my teeth and tried again. I was so frustrated that I spoke to the presence in the room, "I am justified in doing what I am doing. Why are you trying to stop me?" As an answer to my question, I became weak and fell like a dead person. I felt layers of obstruction to my vision being removed like scales falling from the eyes of a blind man. I was taken into the presence of a great white light. I could see beautiful rivers of light. At that time, I could see and know many things. I could also see the earth, and myself lying still on the earth. At that time, I was so consumed with the idea of dying that the awesomeness of what I was experiencing didn't strike me.

Then the light communicated to me. This message came to the center of my being. It was not a voice, but something very different. It was not even in English or any other languages known to me, although I am describing it in English now. It came with power like thousands of volts of electricity and I thought that I would burst. I heard a voice that said, "We know what you are going through, but this is not what we expect from you. We want you to stand! Stand! Stand!" But I could not understand the meaning of "stand" in this context. I pointed to myself on the earth and said, "See? This person cannot live. The thing that makes a person live is gone from him." Again the message continued, "I give you a new life and also I will give you a song to comfort you." I was shown a big hand under me, which prevented my falling. I felt something being poured into me like water into a test tube. When that pouring reached up to my head, I felt the strong negativity subside and I was back in my room.

I tried to make sense of what I had experienced but could not, so I decided that some higher soul had taken a special interest in me. At the time, I found a verse in the Bible, which summarizes the description of the hand I saw under me. When I repeat this verse from the Bible, "Eternal God is thy refuge and underneath are the everlasting arms" [Deuteronomy 33:27], I always find strength and thank God for his mercies.

Author

Johnson's experience changed his life forever and allowed him to see that he is not alone, even in the most desperate of situations. He felt a presence that showed him his life from another perspective, an out-of-body perspective, as well as the value of his existence.

Johnson had experienced "the light," something that I have found through extensive research that many people are increasingly experiencing. This occurrence always includes being in the presence of, and filled with, the light. Also experienced is immediate insight and a perspective that is often incomprehensible in the beginning. In addition, the body goes into the state of partial or complete paralysis while light surges through the physical body, allowing you to experience life from a heightened perspective. While in this state of heightened perspective, visions and spontaneous information stream through your consciousness and you immediately become aware of the healing capabilities available to you. After you have received these visions and spontaneous information, your world becomes as vast as you allow it to become. Even if we are not able to make sense of our paranormal healing experiences, we can never doubt their heavenly origin once we have experienced for ourselves healings of a paranormal nature.

Chapter 15
Evolution

"Man is not a being who stands still, he is a being in
the process of becoming. The more he enables himself
to become, the more he fulfills his true mission."
—*Rudolph Steiner*

When we talk about evolution, normally we do so from a perspective of time. Time, as you know it here on earth, is a manufactured concept used to regulate your experiences and existence while you are in a physical and earthly form.

When we discuss the growth of our spirit, we might be wise
to consider that time is nonexistent, and that the past, present,
and future are all happening simultaneously, and at different
frequencies felt as levels of vibration. Though this concept may
be difficult for the mind to comprehend, it is nevertheless the
truth in all matters where the evolution of our consciousness is
concerned. Our consciousness needs no physical body to
evolve; therefore, consciousness has no use for, and is not relative to, physical time.

What is evolution, and what does it have to do with our soul?
The evolution of the soul is the process of reawakening and remembering that you are made of light. It is the continual process of stirring the spirit of God within you. It is shedding any
misconceptions and false perceptions that began to influence
you shortly after the time of creation. These influences, some-

times indistinguishable, come to us in every form for the purpose of soul advancement.

Influences that can govern, and sometimes prevent the lack of our evolution, have always been present since our beginning. These influences, created as necessary tools for our evolution, are looked upon today as forces opposing the light. If we look at our lives from the perspective of evolving back to the light, then it is also important to look at the nature of darkness and its influences upon our evolution.

How did opposing forces that influence our lives begin? It is believed in the Judeo-Christian religious tradition that an angel named Lucifer, the most beautiful of all the archangels, was rebellious against the authority of God and thrown from the heavens to rule in hell for eternity. However, we might ask ourselves, if God is merciful, why would he cast his own creations to eternal hell?

If we look at the name Lucifer, we will see that Lucifer derives from the Latin term *lucem ferre*, meaning bringer or bearer of light.

Lucifer has been coined "the fallen angel" for his rebellion and refusal to give in to the light and state of oneness in which he was made, but held no power over. His desire for power, and his retaliation, no longer made him suitable for the heavens. This marked the beginning point of karma and thus began the balance between good versus evil within our human experiences.

Lucifer, responsible for all negative forces from a heavenly standpoint, actually aids humanity in ways unseen by offering choices and opportunities on a continual basis to make correct and wise decisions concerning our lives. If we did not have this diversity, there would not be the necessity for choice.

Diversity, good versus evil, not only offers us a vista to our higher perceptions, but also the continual opportunity to utilize these perceptions as opportunities for growth. Both are beneficial and necessary to our spiritual evolution.

Those who have chosen a negative path in life are without the understanding that their light within is simply bound by darkness. How do we detect negative or dark energy? We do this by first recognizing a feeling that we are not comfortable with, and then we pay attention to what it is that is causing our spiritual red flags to appear. Once we know what it is that causes us discomfort, we can eliminate it from our lives.

Why does darkness appear as light? It is to test your progression. When we once again are back to a state of complete unification—and we are moving toward this now—there will no longer be the necessity for the deceptions of darkness and the lessons in balancing that our experiences bring.

If we believe that God truly forgives, and that we are all connected to everything in creation, then we might consider that no one will be left out when the moment of our complete ascension arrives. It is also wise to consider that Lucifer may have volunteered to help humanity by using temptations of every sort to bring forth, in clarity, the difference between darkness and light so that we may better be able to discover that which keeps us from our evolution.

If you are unsure about any situation in life, ask yourself, "Is this light or dark?" It is as easy at that. When you receive your answer, try not to go against your first inclination. If there were no truth to first inclinations—strong currents of energy that best serve us—then we would not have them.

The lessons provided by Lucifer at this time are lessons in envy, jealousy, lust, hatred, control, anger, and everything else that falls under negative experiences designed for maximum spiritual growth. If this darkness around us did not exist, we would not have the desire to search for the light.

As we progress throughout lifetimes, our energy is constantly changing. As we continue to evolve, we not only become sensitive to others in a way we may have never experienced before, we may also notice visual changes within our perceptional fields. We may look around at different people and begin to recognize that we can actually see light radiating from some human beings more than others. This does not mean that a person is more spiritually progressed, it simply means that the level and frequency within your energy field is heightening.

The changes you can expect as you evolve to higher states of consciousness include not only the ability to see light within others, but also the ability to recognize different energy frequencies. This is due to the momentum caused by the creation of light from energy. As you become clear of all physically and emotionally blocked energy in your life, the molecular mobility of your energy begins to move at a faster rate. This not only creates emanating and radiating light perceptible to the human eye, but also an audible sound, a vibration, that is much like that of a hum. This hum is recognizable to others who reside on the same level of vibration as you.

Energy frequencies are important because they are your stepping-stones to ascension. Your current energy level and understanding of this energy greatly reflects both your perceptions in life and your life experiences.

When two people come together, and one resides on a lower energy frequency, in order to communicate, a person must adjust their energy pattern in order to meet another's, much the same as spirits do in order to communicate with you. This is why it is important to maintain good company, so that negative influences—anything that slows your evolutional progression—do not sway your life's decisions.

In life, arrays of choices are continually presented to us at every moment. You will find that when you have made a good and wise choice, everything will easily fall into place. When you have made an unwise choice, most assuredly obstacles will be placed in your path that will seem to slow your progression. This is how you know whether you are going in the right direction. If you are unsure, look to see how your life is going.

How can we change our lives? We can begin by changing our thoughts and speech, which lay the foundations for our created experiences. Once we become aware that we can create change within our own life experiences by changing our thoughts, we can then make all corrections and adjustments necessary to lead to a fruitful life.

What is the ultimate objective in our evolution? The ultimate objective is to love completely. If you are now moving toward a life direction that does not include *love*, the place from which we were created, and you can almost feel yourself shrinking from the very thought of it, you must remember that to love is a decision. It is *your* decision. It is your decision to allow the expression of that of which you already are, but may have forgotten, to come forth. You are the God-created expression of Himself. From this point of view, all things are possible.

How do we create love in our lives if we feel we do not have it? If you should decide that love would be your state of being at all times, then love is what you will experience. It is as easy as plugging in a light and turning it on, but first you must make the decision to do so.

Through our many earthly incarnations, showing love to our fullest capacity is not always an easy task. When we recognize this, that we may not have love in our lives, or love ourselves as anyone could hope to, it is wise to remember that we have created all situations that we experience. These experiences offer us the opportunity to love to our fullest capacity possible. When you cross over, you will immediately see how well you passed through all opportunities presented in life in order to move closer to love.

What is important to remember during your evolutional journey through this lifetime? One of the most important questions you will be faced with directly after death is "How did you make others feel?" What is important in life are not the kind gestures that you bestow upon another, though they are valuable lessons in giving. What matters is how these gestures of giving, in any form, are received. In other words, when you give of yourself, make certain that you are giving out of love and for the benefit of someone else and not just for you. This is true giving, edifying another in a way that touches upon all beings.

Evolution is rising to meet the unseen forces of our divinity, which lead us closer to remembering when we held complete consciousness; a time void of any negative experiences, and a time when there was no you and I, but there was *us*. Evolution is recalling a time when we were able to feel the full capacity of love, and how this love was void of all separation, as it was at the moment of our creation.

Conclusion

"If I speak in the tongues of men and of angels, but have not love, I am only a resounding gong or a clanging cymbal. If I have the gift of prophecy and can fathom all mysteries and all knowledge, and if I have a faith that can move mountains, but have not love, I am nothing. If I give all I possess to the poor and surrender my body to the flames, but have not love I gain nothing. Love is patient, love is kind. It does not envy, it does not boast, it is not proud. It is not rude, it is not self-seeking, it is not easily angered, it keeps no record of wrongs. Love does not delight in evil but rejoices with the truth. It always protects, always trusts, always perseveres. Love never fails. But where there are prophecies, they will cease; where there are tongues, they will be stilled; where there is knowledge, it will pass away.

And now these things remain: faith, hope and love. But the greatest of these is love."

—1 Corinthians 13:1–13, *Holy Bible*

Suggested Reading

Cayce, Hugh Lynn, and Edgar Cayce. *No Death: God's Other Door*. Virginia Beach, VA: A.R.E. Publishing, Inc., 1999.

Martin, Joel and Romanowski, Patricia. *Love beyond Life: The Healing Power of After-Death Communications*. New York: Bantam Doubleday Dell Publishing Group, Inc., 1998.

Moody, Raymond A., M.D. *Life After Life*. Atlanta: Mockingbird Books, 1975.

Morse, Melvin, M.D., with Paul Perry. *Closer to the Light: Learning from the Near-Death Experiences of Children*. Ivy Books, 1991.

Newton, Michael, PhD. *Destiny of the Souls: New Case Studies of Life Between Lives*. St. Paul, MN: Llewellyn Publications, 2000.

Stevenson, Ian, M.D. *Children Who Remember Previous Lives: A Question of Reincarnation*. Charlottesville: University Press of Virginia, 1987.

ORDER FORM

Order this book, and others at
TranspersonalPublishing.com
or send the following order form in with
__check
__money order
__credit
card_____
exp._____ Zip Code of CCd_____

Afterlifefromabove
_____books at 14.95 =   _____
plus $2/1 copies or $3/2 copies
      Sh&Hdl   _____
NC residents at 8% sales tax   _____

                          Total due_____

Make checks and money orders payable to
Transpersonal Publishing
P.O. Box 7220
Kill Devil Hills, NC 27948

*All shipping is U.S., and must be media mail.
Phone for priority or international shipping
800-296-MIND. Free shipping for 3 or more copies.
Prices and availability subject to change without notice.

Or visit:
http://www.geocities.com/afterlifefromabove/
Author's e-mail: Afterlifefromabove@yahoo.com